ISBN 978-0-259-89531-2
PIBN 10000447

1 MONTH OF
FREE
READING

at

www.ForgottenBooks.com

By purchasing this book you are eligible for one month membership to ForgottenBooks.com, giving you unlimited access to our entire collection of over 1,000,000 titles via our web site and mobile apps.

To claim your free month visit:

www.forgottenbooks.com/free447

English
Français
Deutsche
Italiano
Español
Português

www.forgottenbooks.com

Mythology Photography **Fiction**
Fishing Christianity **Art** Cooking
Essays Buddhism Freemasonry
Medicine **Biology** Music **Ancient
Egypt** Evolution Carpentry Physics
Dance Geology **Mathematics** Fitness
Shakespeare **Folklore** Yoga Marketing
Confidence Immortality Biographies
Poetry **Psychology** Witchcraft
Electronics Chemistry History **Law**
Accounting **Philosophy** Anthropology
Alchemy Drama Quantum Mechanics
Atheism Sexual Health **Ancient History**
Entrepreneurship Languages Sport
Paleontology Needlework Islam
Metaphysics Investment Archaeology
Parenting Statistics Criminology
Motivational

Mental Therapeutics

OR

Just How To Heal Oneself And Others

By THERON Q. DUMONT

Author of "Personal Magnetism"; "Practical Memory Training"; "Power to Concentrate"; etc., etc.

INCLUDING

THE LATEST AND BEST METHODS OF PRESENT AND DISTANT MENTAL HEALING

ADVANCED THOUGHT PUBLISHING CO.
CHICAGO, ILL.

L. N. FOWLER & CO.
7 Imperial Arcade, Ludgate Circus, London, Eng.

TABLE OF CONTENTS

LESSON I
THE SCIENCE OF MENTAL HEALING

Mental Therapeutics a Science, not a superstition. Natural, not supernatural. Not a theology or a religion. Mind is Unknowable, but its activities are known and may be intelligently applied. How Mind may be harnessed to do work for us. A rational system of mental hygiene, based upon the known laws of mind and matter. The essence of the best teaching..............Pages 7–14

LESSON II
THE CORPOREAL MIND

The body is the organ of the mind. Mind over mind; not Mind over Matter. The Corporeal Mind is the "bodily mind," consisting of a unity of cell-minds, and organ-minds. A phase of the Subconscious Mind. The Corporeal Mind is amenable to suggestion. What Suggestion is, and the laws of its manifestation. ....Pages 15–22

LESSON III
THE CELLS OF THE BODY

The human body is composed of minute cells. What these cells are, and of what they are composed. The cells are individual and separate, yet work by combining and co-operating. Forty kinds of cells, and what they do. The body a great co-operative community of cells. The wonderful story of the cells, and the manifold activities manifested by them...............Pages 23–30

LESSON IV
MIND IN THE CELLS

Each cell is alive, and possesses a mind of its own. Group-mind of cell communities. Telepathic communication between the cells and groups. The psychology of the cell-minds. Disease is the failure of the cells to function properly. Cures are made by reaching the mind in the cells, and cell-groups, and inducing them to function normally........................Pages 31–38

LESSON V
THE SYMPATHETIC NERVOUS SYSTEM

The intricate nervous system by which the Corporeal Mind reaches all parts of its kingdom. What the Sympathetic Nervous System is, and how it operates. How it performs the unconscious and involuntary functions and offices of the body. How it conducts the nutritive and reparative work. The Ganglia; the Plexi; the Abdominal Brain..............................Pages 39–46

LESSON VI
MENTAL CAUSE OF DISEASE

How improper thought and mental states cause disease. Why Fear is contagious. How persons have become ill and have died by reason of fright and fearthought. How the Corporeal Mind exercises control over the nervous, vaso-motor, circulatory and other systems of the body. How imagination has caused serious diseases. How to reach the root of disease..........Pages 47–54

LESSON VII
THE FUNDAMENTAL PRINCIPLE OF CURE

All forms of cure of disease are really phases of Mental Healing. The Vis Medicatrix Naturae. The defensive and reparative forces of the body are mental forces. The life process acting through the cells performs the cure; and this process is purely mental in nature. How the Corporeal Mind energizes the cells and cell-groups under proper mental stimulus.......Pages 55-62

LESSON VIII
THE HISTORY OF MENTAL THERAPEUTICS

An interesting story of the history of Mental Healing. How the ancient priests and magicians employed the principle. How Mental Healing was incorporated with religions. The healing virtues of shrines, relics, holy places, religious ceremonies, etc., and the principle behind them. The history of Christian Science and New Thought...................................Pages 63-71

LESSON IX
DISGUISED MENTAL HEALING

How the principle of Mental Healing has been employed under many strange disguises. The psychology of cures by the imagination. The placebos of the physicians, and why they perform cures. How physicians fool themselves and others. The Hack Tuke experiments, and their explanation. Why patent medicines cure. The Key to the Puzzle...........................Pages 72-79

LESSON X
THREE METHODS OF MENTAL HEALING

Healing by Mental Suggestion. Healing by Present Thought Induction. Healing by Distant Thought Induction. The principles involved in each, and the distinction between them. All operate by arousing into renewed and normal activity and functioning the mind in the cells, organs, and parts of the body of the patient. How these methods may be combined.......Pages 80-87

LESSON XI
MENTAL SUGGESTION

The basis of Mental Suggestion. What a Suggestion is, and how it acts upon the subconscious mind. The psychology of Suggestion. The mental factors employed in Suggestion. Earnest Attention in Suggestion. Expectant Attention in Suggestion. Pleasurable Mental States in Suggestion. The dynamic force of Attention. The power of Expectancy.................Pages 88-95

LESSON XII
PRINCIPLES OF SUGGESTION

The leading principles of Suggestion. How the principle of Authority operates in Suggestion. How the principle of Association operates in Suggestion. How the principle of Earnestness operates in Suggestion. How the principle of Repetition operates in Suggestion. How to manifest the mental attitude of Authority in giving suggestive treatments................ ..Pages 96-103

LESSON XIII
THERAPEUTIC SUGGESTION

How to reach the mind of the patient by Suggestion. The best channels of influence. How to diagnose the mental and emotional characteristics of patients. How to apply the appropriate methods to fit each case. How to suggest to the "religious type" of patients, the "metaphysical type;" the "psychological type;" the "new thing" type; so as to get the best results.....Pages 104-112

LESSON XIV
WHAT TO SUGGEST TO PATIENTS

How to paint the pictures of the desired result. How to arouse the expectant attention of the patient. General suggestions of health, and specific suggestions to fit the particular cases. The "rifle-bullet" treatment and the "shot-gun" treatment; how to combine both. How to "reach the spot" and avoid "scatteration." How to reach the cell-minds......................Pages 113–120

LESSON XV
THERAPEUTIC AUTO-SUGGESTION
What Auto-Suggestion is, and how it resembles ordinary Suggestion. How to suggest to one's own body, parts, cells, and organs. The philosophy and psychology of Auto-Suggestion, or Self-Healing. The methods of eminent teachers and healers. How to reach your Inner Consciousness by Auto-Suggestion. How to treat the organs of your body, and to heal them..Pages 121–128

LESSON XVI
THOUGHT INDUCTION
What Thought Induction really is. How to employ Thought Induction in healing. How mental states, feelings, and thoughts tend to induce similar activities in other minds, without direct contact. The strange correspondence between Thought and Electricity. Thought is radio-active. Thought transformation and transmission, without conducting mediums........Pages 129–136

LESSON XVII
THE PRACTICE OF THOUGHT INDUCTION
How to induce thought vibrations in the minds of others. Exercise for practice and development of the power. How to transform words into thought-vibrations. How to arouse the Corporeal Mind of the patient by Thought Induction. Full directions for actual practice. How to produce the desired psychological condition and state......................Pages 137–144

LESSON XVIII
DISTANT THOUGHT INDUCTION
How to treat patients at a distance by Thought Induction. "Absent Healing" explained, scientifically. Mental "Wireless" an established fact of science. Telepathy an accepted principle. How mind affects mind at a distance. How the transformation of a psychic action into an ethereal movement, and the reverse, is accomplished ....Pages 145–152

LESSON XIX
HOW THOUGHT TRAVELS TO A DISTANCE
How to establish mental lines of communication between the practitioner and his patient. How Thought travels along ethereal lines of its own making, until it reaches the receiving mind attuned to it. How Thought projects from itself the lines over which it travels to a distance. How you build the mental track by thinking it into existence......................Pages 153–160

LESSON XX
HOW TO HEAL AT A DISTANCE
Directions for preparing the mind of the patient for the treatment. Cautions to the patient to prevent influx of undesirable thought-waves. Establishing the rapport condition. The feeling of "closeness." Visualizing the patient's presence. How to begin the Distant Treatment; how to conduct it; and how to close it. A typical illustrative case, and treatment..Pages 161–168

LESSON XXI
THE PHYSIOLOGY OF MENTAL HEALING
A basic knowledge of physiology required in order that the normal conditions may be visualized and manifested into reality. A mental pattern of normal health and function must be created. All healing consists in restoring Nature's normal rule and operations. How Nature performs her healing work. How to call into operation Nature's Forces......................Pages 169–176

5

LESSON XXII
THE NUTRITIVE PROCESSES

How Nature nourishes the body, and builds-up, repairs, and sustains it by taking the nourishment contained in the blood How the nourishment gets into the blood from the food The activities of the stomach. The activities of the small intestine The part played by the liver, pancreas, etc. How the nourishment is absorbed into the blood. A great lesson.........Pages 177-184

LESSON XXIII
THE ELIMINATIVE PROCESSES

How Nature eliminates the waste products and debris of the system, and disposes of its garbage. The elimination by the breath; by the skin; by the kidneys; and by the bowels How the sweat and urine carry off waste. The work of the Colon, or large bowel; the great sewer of the system. How to restore natural conditions of these organs. A valuable lesson.......Pages 185-192

LESSON XXIV
"THE BLOOD IS THE LIFE"

How Nature provides a canal system for carrying nourishment to all parts of the body, and carrying off refuse and garbage. What the blood is. What the arteries and veins are, and what they do. The part played by the heart. How the blood is "liquid flesh" destined to become solid flesh. Why the blood is "the life" of the body..............................Pages 193-202

LESSON XXV
THE REPRODUCTIVE SYSTEM

How Nature performs her work of reproduction, and preservation of the race. The Reproductive Organism of the Male. The nature of each organ, and the part it performs. The Spermatozoa, or "living seed," and how they act. The Reproductive Organism of the Female. The nature of each organ, and the part it performs...Pages 203-212

LESSON XXVI
"WHEN THE HAND OF THE POTTER SLIPS"

When Nature fails in her full purpose; and how to help her to complete her work, and how to restore it when damaged. Full directions for General Treatment. Also full directions for special treatments of the following classes of diseases: Troubles of the Organs of Nutrition; of the Organs of Elimination; of the Heart and Circulation; of the Lungs; Rheumatic troubles; troubles of the Sense-Organs; Neuralgic troubles, and Headaches; troubles of the Reproductive System; Nervous troubles, etc. Treatment of others, and Self-treatment. Valuable Advice.... ....Pages 213-224

LESSON XXVII
MAGNETIC AND SPIRITUAL HEALING

The principles of Magnetic Healing fully explained. How to perform Magnetic Healing effectively. The effect of the different kind of passes. A common-sense, scientific explanation of the subject of Spiritual Healing, which includes the highest conceptions of the best authorities......................Pages 225-232

LESSON I

THE SCIENCE OF MENTAL HEALING

In these lessons I shall give you the essence and substance of the best scientific knowledge regarding the prevention and cure of physical ills by the power of the mind.

But in presenting the theory and practice of Mental Therapeutics to you I shall carefully avoid all reference to mysticism or occultism, or strange metaphysical and philosophical theories. Mental Therapeutics is a science, not a superstition; it is something based on sound scientific facts, and not upon vague imaginings.

Nature surely contains enough wonders for us, without the need of our exploring any so-called supernatural realms in our search for the relief of the ills and pains of mankind. The Power that has called us into being has placed at our disposal many wonderful means of self-help, and self-cure. There is no need for us to become "spooky" or uncanny when we begin the study of Mental Therapeutics, nor when we carry the theory into the realm of actual practice. There are greater wonders and mysteries wrapped up in the domain of Nature than have ever been dreamed of by man in his search for the supernatural.

Neither is there any need of dragging the religious element into Mental Therapeutics, for it has no direct connection with the scientific side of the subject. There is no one who has a greater, deeper, or more profound respect, veneration, and reverence than have I for the Power which is back of all Nature, and which is yet manifest in every one of her activities. Moreover, I firmly believe that a firm faith in that Power has an uplifting effect upon the minds and souls of persons, and therefore tends to keep them in health, and to restore health when it has been lost. But, I believe that theology and Mental Therapeutics are two distinct fields of human thought and activity. I do not believe in making a religion of Mental Therapeutics, and of mixing theological doctrines with the scientific methods of applying the latter.

In fact, while many persons have received benefit from Mental Therapeutics administered under the guise and form of religious teaching, I also believe that many more persons have been repelled and kept away from the wonderful benefits of this form of treatment by reason of the strange and queer theological teachings of some of the healers. There is no reason in the world why any person should forsake his or her chosen religion—the faith that has been of such great comfort and consolation to him or her during many years of life—in order to obtain the benefits of the "new" healing methods. Rather do I believe that the best therapeutic methods of this new system may be applied with the best results when the patient is supported by the comforting assurance of his or her own chosen faith

THE SCIENCE OF MENTAL HEALING

Under the guise of mental healing many persons have been induced to forsake the faith of their fathers, and the faith of their youth; too often with the result that they have become like ships without a rudder, drifting and floating backward and forward with every passing current. These people have let go of the old, without getting a firm hold on the new. At the last, all religion may be summed up in three general principles, viz.: (1) Belief in the existence of a Supreme Being or Power, from whom all life proceeds; (2) faith in, and dependence upon, the goodness of that Being or Power in all the affairs and circumstances of daily life; and (3) living the Right Life, in accord with the highest teachings of the best faiths, and in accordance with the dictates of one's own conscience. Having these principles, and living up to them as closely as one can, one is truly religious, no matter what his faith or profession.

So, my students, in these lessons you will not be torn away from the safe anchorage of your religious faith, nor asked to accept some strange and new theology as a precedent to your learning the art and science of healing yourself and others. While, as I have said, all thinking men recognize the presence and being of a Supreme Power, and seek assistance and aid from, and depend upon it accordingly; still we shall find that this Supreme Power has placed within our grasp the means and methods whereby we may study and practice this science, as we would any other science. Mental Therapeutics is neither a religion, nor a theology; it is a scientific system of healing by natural means and methods.

Moreover, although Mind is the great force and power with which cures are made under the system of Mental Therapeutics, we shall not be asked to accept any particular metaphysical theory of "What is Mind?" We do not insist upon teachers of physical science telling us exactly what Matter is! The truth is that they do not know; neither does any one else know. And, likewise, no one knows just what Mind is; nor are they likely to know. Mind, Matter, and Energy—these are the three great manifestations of the Supreme Power; and it has pleased that Supreme Power to render them perhaps forever unknown to us in their final nature. The sanest attitude to take toward these mysteries is that of Herbert Spencer, i. e., that Mind, Matter, and Energy are the threefold aspects of the manifestation of that "Infinite and Eternal Power" from which all things proceed; and which, like the Power that has called them into being, is Unknowable at the last.

But, while we do not know "just what Mind is," we most assuredly do know just how it works. Like electricity, the nature of which we do not know either, we have harnessed Mind to do work for us. We have in Mind a wonderful and most potent force or natural energy, and we have learned how to guide, direct, and apply its energies and power in the direction of the healing of physical ills. We have discovered that Mind works as regularly, and as surely, as does electricity. And we know that we may set it to work in special direction, surely and invariably, when we provide the channels for its expression.

As we proceed with these lessons, we shall discover also that not only does Mind prevent and cure diseases, but that it also causes diseases. Fear has slain more human beings than the most malignant fever. Its victims are numbered by the millions. And not only does it kill, but it cripples and incapacitates millions, and renders them miserable and unable to live normal lives and to perform efficient work for themselves and those dependent upon them. Like all other great forces, Mind acts negatively as well as positively—it harms as well as benefits. Wisdom consists in learning its laws and principles of operation; and thereby learning to prevent its undesirable working, and to encourage, cultivate and direct its beneficent activities.

In these lessons I shall try to bring order out of chaos in mental healing. There has been so much ill-digested teaching on the subject, and so much fanciful and often absurd theorizing, that the intelligent student is often perplexed when he begins the study thereof.

A writer upon this subject, in a recent magazine article, has well said: "Past teaching respecting the influence of the mind upon the body has been clouded and distorted by the errors of superstition, the inaccuracies of ignorance, and the exaggeration of fanatical extremists whose prejudiced observations and reports were more or less colored by commercial motives or sectarian enthusiasm. And so it was no little wonder that teaching mental healing grew into a mass of religious contradictions, unreliable observations, and groundless assertions. It has required much painstaking labor on the part of modern physiologists and psychologists to clear away this accumulation of rubbish and ignorance, and to lay a scientific foundation for a rational system of mental hygiene based upon the known laws of mind and matter.''

The student will notice that in these lessons I have not confined myself solely to the psychology of Mental Therapeutics. I have accepted the facts of modern physiology as correct; and have directed the use of the power of the mind along the lines of these physiological facts. One of the great mistakes of unscientific practitioners of mental healing has been the fact that they have refused to accept physiology as existent; but have used the mind in a general hit-or-miss fashion. The scientific practitioner, on the contrary, acquaints himself with the physiology of the normal person, and then bends the mental energies toward restoring this normal state and condition of functioning. By knowing just how the organs of the body function in health, the practitioner is better able to picture in the mind of the patient (and in his own mind) exactly what conditions are desired to be created. As the mental picture is the pattern around which Mind creates, it will be seen that the importance of creating the right kind of mental pattern cannot be overestimated. There is a great truth of Mental Therapeutics stated here; and the student will do well to make note of it.

But, while we shall be led into the study of elementary physiology in connection with the psychology of cure, we shall not be bothered with technical scientific terms. Wherever possible these technical terms shall be discarded. When it is impossible to proceed without them we shall explain them in simple terms, so that any person of average intelligence will be able to understand them. True knowledge does not consist of a parrot-like memorizing or repetition of long words, or foreign terms; rather does it consist of an understanding of the real meaning of the things described; particularly as regards the question of "how they work."

I ask my students, here at the very beginning, to lay aside all preconceived ideas and acquired prejudices. Not that they must accept my theories and methods in preference to their own, regardless of the comparative value thereof; but rather that they should cultivate an open mind to what I have to say, until they are able to grasp the why and wherefore of it. In some cases they may think that I mean something quite different from my real meaning; this by reason of their unfamiliarity with my terms. We all have our own terms, and we are suspicious of new ones. Therefore, we should always be sure that we really understand the real meaning of the terms used by others.

Finally, we must once and for all get rid of the idea that Truth is the exclusive possession of any one school of thought or practice. There is a little good in almost all schools and methods; and the most good is always obtained by analyzing the different theories and methods, and then taking the essence of all that is best, discarding the waste material. This is the true scientific method—the "eclectic" method, combining the best of the many forms and phases examined; selecting the best in each, and combining this in one general system and method. Any other plan results in narrowness and bigotry, both of which is quite unscientific, and quite contrary to common sense.

Having now understood the methods and general plan of these lessons, let us now proceed to investigate, examine, and understand the working principles and the basic theories of this great system of the healing art—Mental Therapeutics.

LESSON II

THE CORPOREAL MIND

One of the first things that the student of Mental Therapeutics should learn is this: That the human body is not a mass of mindless matter, but is, instead, as truly an organ of the mind as is the brain, although its mental work is along different lines. This may seem like a startling statement to the person who has not acquainted himself with the discoveries of modern psychology and physiology.

Not only is the body as a whole the outward aspect of an inward mentality, but every part of it (even the cells themselves) has mind immanent within it and acting through it. And, more than this, every part has its own particular mental nature; and every cell its own mental being. There is no part of the body, no organ of the body, no cell of the body, that is without its own mental being or nature.

When this important fact is perceived, the fundamental explanation of mental healing is had. The student then no longer speaks of the power of "mind over matter," for he sees that it is really a manifestation of **mind over mind**—of one kind of mind over another kind of mind. This fact being grasped thoroughly, the whole system of mental cure is perceived as a reasonable and logical idea, instead of a theory opposed to the accepted facts of Nature.

Just as the activities of the brain-cells in

performing their own allotted work are so closely correlated and combined that they are regarded as a unity, and form our thinking "mind" as a whole; so are the activities of our cells, parts, organs and members of our bodies so closely correlated and combined in their actions and interaction that they form a unity, and may be regarded as one mind working in harmony and unity. For the want of a better name this combined mind may be called **"The Corporeal Mind."** This term will be used in these lessons to indicate this great indwelling mind which is the active spirit of our physical functions and bodily life.

The term "corporeal" means: "pertaining to a material body." Therefore Corporeal Mind means "the bodily mind." As we proceed we shall discover the qualities, properties, and attributes of the Corporeal Mind.

The Corporeal Mind, however, must not be thought of as dwelling apart and separate from the other fields of mental activity which exist in every person. In fact, no part or field of activity in the human being, whether physical or psychical, so dwells apart; everything is correlated, interdependent, and interactive—all coordinated and harmonious parts of one whole.

The Corporeal Mind is really one of the phases or planes of that great field of human mentality known as the Subconscious Mind. The Subconscious Mind performs about eighty percent of the mental activity of the person; the remaining twenty percent being left for the Conscious

Mind to perform. Just as the Conscious Mind consists and is composed of the many faculties of sensation, perception, thought, etc., so is the Subconscious Mind composed of numerous distinct planes or fields of subconscious mental activity. The many excellent works on the Subconscious Mind have given the world full information regarding the activities of this great field or plane of mentality. It is not necessary for us to consider the general subject here; so we shall confine ourselves to merely that part of the Great Subconsciousness that relates to the functions of the human body, i. e., the Corporeal Mind.

But, in our consideration of the subject we must not omit the consideration of the important fact that the Corporeal Mind, like all other phases or aspects of the Subconscious Mind, responds to the ideas, suggestions, and orders given it by the Conscious Mind of its owner. And, also it "takes up," or accepts the ideas, suggestions, or commands of the minds of others, unless its owner orders it not to do so. This important psychological fact explains the undoubted occurrence of the causing of disease by the accepted ideas and suggestions of others, or of one's own conscious mind; and, likewise, the cure and removal of disease by the same causes.

Before proceeding to the consideration of the details of the nature of the Corporeal Mind, it will be best for us to consider this fact of the acceptance of the ideas and suggestions, or autosuggestions, by the Corporeal Mind, and its response thereto. It is always well to become acquainted with the general principles and laws before proceeding to the study of their detailed and particular manifestations.

There are several general laws which govern the activities of the Subconscious Mind, which are found to manifest universally, and which therefore may always be expected to exert their influence. These laws are as follows:

I. The Subsconscious Mind accepts as true any idea suggested to it, or impressed upon it; **unless** (a) there already exists in the Subconscious Mind a contrary idea sufficiently strong to counteract the new one; or (b) the Subconscious Mind has acquired a certain mental trend, or habit of thought, which is opposed to the introduction of the new idea; or (c) the Subconscious Mind is **commanded** by its owner not to receive or accept such suggestions or ideas, or classes of ideas.

II. The Subconscious Mind proceeds to logically manifest the conclusion of the suggested and accepted idea; to make it take form in action or physical condition; to adopt it as a habit of manifestation and action, thereafter.

III. The Subconscious Mind will continue to manifest along the lines of the accepted suggested idea until either (a) it is neutralized, cancelled, and replaced by a sufficiently strong opposing idea or suggestion; or (b) the accepted suggested idea is traced back to its birth in the mind of the person, and is thereupon shown to be erroneous, based on wrong premises, and therefore untrue; in both of which cases it is wiped from the tablets of the mind, and cease to manifest—or, to be more exact, it is thus **painted over** by the new and true idea, and ceases to appear in the mind, or to manifest in action or form.

The student is cautioned against regarding the term "Suggestion" to mean any mysterious use of the mind; or as being confined to certain forms of ideas. The term "suggestion" means merely "an indirect or guarded mode of presenting an idea, especially an argument or piece of advice." It is distinguished from argument, or logical proof, by the absence of formal evidence or discussion. A suggestion is usually merely **an idea which seems plausible, and which is advanced with an air or appearance of truth, reality, or accepted fact.** An "auto-suggestion" is a suggestion advanced by the conscious mind of the person himself, usually derived from the "working over" of ideas which he has heard but which were not accepted at the time; although when the person is acquainted with the psychology of suggestion he may deliberately form ideas which he deliberately "auto-suggests" to his Subconscious Mind as facts.

Ideas are suggested and accepted by the Subconscious Mind in a number of ways, of which the following are the most important classes:

(1) Authority. Persons are strongly affected by ideas suggested with an air or appearance of authority. Persons exercising authority, such as priests and preachers, teachers and instructors, physicians, lawyers, judges, persons in charge of and directing other men, writers, public speakers, etc., manifest an appearance of authority, and speak in tones of authority, hence their suggestion carry with them a weight which in many cases is out of all proportion to their truth or real value.

(2) Acquiescence, or Imitation. Persons accept implicitly, in many cases, the ideas of those around them. They imitate the mental states of others, and accept their ideas and belief becomes of the influence of numbers. "Everyone thinks so-and-so" takes the place of proof in their minds. More than this they "take on" the physical conditions of those around them, for the same reason. The Subconscious Mind is quite imitative, and readily falls into the habit of accepting the beliefs, ideas, and conditions of those around its owner.

(3) Association. Persons accept easily suggested ideas which resemble other ideas which they have previously accepted. They associate the new idea with the old one, although there may be little or no resemblance between them. Consequently, shrewd and unscrupulous men sometimes impose upon honest persons in this way, i. e., they make themselves, or their proposition, appear like some other person or proposition which has been satisfactory to the person, and this associated sameness disarms the person and causes him to accept the suggested idea far more readily than he would have otherwise. The confidence man, charlatan, and fakir operates along these lines of suggestion. And, likewise, many persons accept suggestions concerning their physical condition, because of this fancied resemblance to something else, which they otherwise would have refused to notice.

An important law of suggestion is this: **Suggestion gains force by repetition.** The first suggestion may make but little impression; but the same suggestion repeated frequently makes a deeper impression by each repetition; until finally the idea is firmly impressed upon the Subconscious Mind of the person.

We shall not consider the important results of suggestion in general, for we are concerned merely with those which produce physical effects. When the Subconscious Mind accepts suggested ideas relating to physical conditions, functioning, health, etc., it at once passes the idea over to that phase, aspect, or department of its activities that we have called the Corporeal Mind. The Corporeal Mind then proceeds to manifest into reality and physical form and function the idea so placed within it, and which it accepts as truth in absence of opposing ideas.

In this way many persons have developed conditions of disease from purely mental causes, and many have died from the logical development of such diseases. Many persons are made ill from fear and suggestions of contagion and infection. Many persons acquire disease by reason of vivid pictures placed in their minds through reading newspaper descriptions of disease, patent medicine advertisements, etc. It is a fact known to all officials of the medical schools that students frequently "take on" all the symptoms of the diseases they are studying about in their text-books.

And, likewise, the law works with equal force in the opposite direction. For all the cures made by the faith-healers, prayer-curists, divine healers, and other practitioners of the same kind; and by the practitioners of mental therapeutics, suggestive therapy, and similar scientific methods of applying the power of the mind to cure physical ills; are really based upon this fundamental principle. This may seem strange to the student when first stated; but a careful examination of the facts of the case will bring to him such an overwhelming proof of its correctness, that it will seem strange to him that anyone can doubt it.

Remember, though, that Therapeutic Suggestion means simply **the indirect placing of an idea in the Subconscious Mind in such a way that it is accepted as truth, and thereupon manifested in action, form, and functioning by that phase of the Subconscious Mind known as the Corporeal Mind, which has control of the functions and activities of the physical body.**

LESSON III

THE CELLS OF THE BODY

The student of physiology and of psychology cannot expect to have a sound base and foundation for his structure of knowledge unless he becomes thoroughly familiar with the nature and character of the cells of which the entire human body is composed.

The corporeal cells are those very minute elementary structures of which the organic tissues are composed. By tissues is meant the elementary materials, varying in structure and function, which compose the bodily organs, members, and parts. And, consequently, the cell is the physical base of the activity of the Corporeal Mind. So, from the position of both physiology and of psychology the cell is the logical subject of the beginning of study and investigation.

The corporeal cells are very minute; in fact, they are microscopic. From them are built up the muscles, tissues, nerves, blood, bones, hair, and nails. From the hardest enamel of the tooth to the most delicate and soft tissue of the mucous membrane, the human body is found to be composed of cells. And these cells are, for all practical purposes of comparison, identical with the single cells which exist as independent entities or living creatures in the lowest forms of the life scale. So that, at the last, every human body is in reality a great community of cells, grouped and associated, co-ordinated and combined for

23

co-operative work and functioning, yet each a separate living organism.

Each of these cells is nucleated, that is to say it has as it center a nucleus which is the most vital point of its being. The nucleus of the cell is its central life-spot; which may be compared to the yolk of an egg. It is more complex than the general substance of the cell, and seems to contain within itself the essence of the life and being of the cell. The cells reproduce themselves by growth and division; they are born, perform their tasks, give birth to other cells, and then die.

The cells preserve a certain degree of individuality and separateness, though their work is performed by reason of their tendency to combine with other cells into groups, and these into still larger groups, and so on; a constant relation being maintained between the members of each group, and so on until all the cells in the body are considered as a great group connected in all of its parts and divisions.

And now let us take a glance at the work performed by these wonderful little bits of living substance, in their various groupings and association with each other. Physiology recognizes about forty different kinds of cells, yet all belong to the one great family of cells. Their differences are merely such adaptations to function, work and purpose as we might expect; the differentiation having resulted in the course of organic evolution.

For instance, we find the great family of

muscle-cells, which are adapted to their work of contracting the muscles which they compose. Then there are the connective-tissue cells which join together and form the tough fibrous tissue which binds together and protects the various parts of the organism. Then again, we find the bone cells which select, arrange, and set in place the lime material of which the bony parts of the body is composed. Then we find the several group of cells which select and place in position the silicate mineral substances which are needed to form the nails, the hair, and other similar parts of the body. Then there are the gland cells which work industriously to secrete the fluids needed in digestion and similar vital processes. Then we discover the very active family of blood cells the members of which work to build up and repair the various parts of the system, and to do the scavenger work of carrying off the debris of the system to be burned-up by the oxygen in the lungs. And, passing over many equally important families of cells, we finally come to the family of brain and nerve cells, the work of which renders possible all feeling, thinking and acting of the human being.

The cell families of the body are like a great co-operative community, each cell and each group of cells performing its own work in the community, each acting for its own good, and the good of its particular group, and at the same time for the good of the entire body of cells. You must here remember that the body exists only as a body of cells—a great co-operative community of cells. It is not sufficient to say and think that "the body **has** cells," but rather that "the body is a collection of cells," or even "the cells are formed into a body of cells."

Some of the cells are on the active line, while others are held in reserve to be called upon in case of sudden need. Some are stationary, while others remain stationary until called into motion, and a third general class is always moving about; of this moving-about class some make regular trips, while others are rovers and free adventurers, like tramp ships sailing from port to port without making regular trips, between ports.

Some of the cells carry burdens of material from place to place—building material needed by certain stationary cells performing building work. Other cells perform scavenger work, and gather up the garbage of the system. Other cells perform police work, and arrest intruders in the system, often actually locking them up by building a wall around them. Other cells form the army which repels the microbes and germs of disease which have invaded the system. The cells of the nervous system form a living telegraph wire, joining hands (so to speak) and passing along the message from one end of the line to another.

The number of cells in the human body is countless. A faint idea of their almost infinite number may be formed by considering the fact that in each cubic inch of blood there are over 75,000,000,000 (seventy-five thousand million) of the red-blood cells alone, not taking into consideration the millions of other kinds of cells.

The red blood cells travel along in the blood flowing through the arteries and veins; first taking up a supply of oxygen from the lungs, and carrying it through the arteries to the various parts of the body, where they deliver it to the cells requiring it for vital processes. Then, starting on their return journey through the veins, they gather up the waste products of the system, such as the broken down cells which have been used up in their work and which have died; this debris is finally consumed in the crematory of the lungs, and thrown off as carbonic acid gas by the breath. Some of these cells force their way through the wall of the arteries and veins, and through the various tissues of the body, when upon hurried calls for repair work.

In the blood currents there are also other kinds of cells than those just mentioned. For instance, there are the police cells and the army cells which have been previously mentioned. These very important cells patrol the system and arrest or combat the germs and bacteria which are dangerous to the health of the body. The policeman cell meeting one of these disorderly bacterial characters, enmeshes or entangles it so that it cannot escape. He then proceeds to devour it, providing that it is not too large and strong for him; in the latter case he summons other policemen cells to his assistance, and between them they carry the intruder to some part of the body where it may be thrown out of the system. Boils and pimples are manifestations of this ejecting process on the part of these cells.

Other cells are laboratory chemists, and extract from the food the elements needed to manufacture the important juices of the system, such as the gastric juice, pancreatic juices, saliva, bile, etc., and also such other secretions as the milk, etc. Not only do these cells select such elements, but they also actually combine them in the proper proportions for the required chemical work.

But perhaps the busiest classes of cells, and the most numerous, are those whose work it is to continually build up and keep in repair the body as a whole. You must remember that the body is constantly undergoing change; constantly breaking down cells; constantly repairing the damaged places with new cells. Our bodies, in all of their parts, are being continuously made over. All of the work of this kind, whether it be the growth of new hair or finger nails, or the slower processes of other parts of the body, is performed by these minute workers, the cells.

Perhaps as typical, and as interesting an example of this work of the cells, is that of the healing of a wound. Let us consider this, in order that we may have a clear idea of the character and wonderful nature of the work performed by the cells. Here is the process:

First, the body is discovered to be wounded by some outside force. The tissues, and often the glands, muscles and nerves are severed. The wound begins to bleed, and its sides separate. The nerves carry the report of trouble to the brain, and there is sent out a hurry-up call for help at once. The cells rush to the scene of the trouble, like firemen called to a fire; or like the repair wagon called to the scene of a breakdown on the trolley-car line. While they are reaching the scene, the flowing blood washes away the dirt which otherwise might cause infection; the blood finally coagulating and forming a protecting substance resembling glue, which afterward develops into a scab.

The repair cells arriving on the scene at once start to work connecting the tissues by bringing together the sides of the wound, and knitting the tissue-cells together. And here is manifested an almost unbelievable degree of "mind." The cells of the tissues, blood-vessels, etc., on both sides of the wound begin to reproduce themselves with marvellous rapidity, each cell growing and separating itself into two, and these into two, and so on, until there is sufficient material created to do the repair work. These new cells increasing in number reach forward from each side of the wound, until finally meeting they connect with their fellows of the other side. But here note the wonder of the process. The connective-tissue cells connect with the connective-tissue cells on the other side; the blood-vessel cells connect with their own kind on the other side; the nerve cells do likewise; until finally there is a complete bridge built, each various parts of each side being connected with the same kind of parts on the other side.

After this internal repair work is completed, and the connections properly made, then the skin cells start to work and build a new skin over the healed wound. The whole process shows purpositive action, co-ordinated effort, and an undoubted presence of mental direction. It is useless for materialists to speak of mechanical and chemical laws as an explanation of such vital processes as these. The most skeptical observer, if he is honest with himself, is forced to admit that there is manifested the activities of living, thinking, minute creatures, co-ordinated and regulated, directed and guided, by some mental center higher than themselves. It is impossible to doubt this, any more than one would doubt that the work of the bees in the hive is a vital, mental manifestation. It is not enough to call it "instinctive"—for instinct itself is but a name given to one phase of vital, mental activity.

A clear understanding of the mental activities of the cells will go far toward giving us a key to the secret of mental healing.

LESSON IV

MIND IN THE CELLS

In the preceding lesson we have seen the wonderful work performed by the cells of which the human body is composed. Can there be any doubt that these cells are alive and have mind within them? Any other supposition would be ridiculous. The single cells found in the lower stages of animal and vegetable life, which perform even less complicated and complex actions are regarded as living, thinking creatures; then there can be no reason for denying life and mind to these cells which compose the human body, and which constitute a great co-operative community.

Biology teaches us that **every living thing is possessed of sufficient mind to enable it to perform its tasks, and adjust itself to its environment.** Even the tiny cells are possessed of sufficient mind to enable them to preserve their lives, perform their work, and reproduce their species. The cells in the human body have sufficient mind to enable them to seek, select, and absorb their own food, and to move from one place to another in search for it when necessary. Moreover, they have mind enough to enable them to perform the complicated work referred to in the preceding lesson. The intelligence shown in the work of the red blood cells is wonderful, and is an undoubted proof of the existence of a high degree of mind in such cells. And the other work per-

31

formed by the other cells, such as the secretion of fluids, the selection of mineral matter needed for building up bone, hair, and nails, is scarcely less wonderful.

Eminent biologists have conducted careful investigations of the life-activities of these cells, and have discovered some very important facts regarding them. For instance, it is discovered that the cells manifest rudimentary memory, which enables them to profit by experience in the direction of avoiding the recurrence of some unpleasant happening. They show their likes and dislikes very plainly; and they exhibit the tendency to acquire habits. Some investigators insist that they even show evidence of purpositive preparation for future action, and act in anticipation of such future necessity.

Binet, the eminent psychologist, in his important work entitled "The Psychic Life of Micro-Organisms," says: "We shall not regard it as strange, perhaps, to find so complete a psychology in the history of the lower organisms, when we call to mind that, agreeably to the ideas of evolution now accepted, a higher animal is nothing more than a colony of protozoans. Every one of the cells composing such an animal has retained its primitive properties, giving them a higher degree of perfection by division of labor and by selection. The epithelial cells that secrete the nails and hair are organisms perfected with reference to the secretion of protective parts. Similarly, the cells of the brain are organisms that have been perfected with reference to psychical attributes."

But the mind in the cells is more than merely the particular manifestation of mind in each particular cell. There is also found a sympathetic and co-ordinated mental activity existing between all the individual cells of the body. There is found what has been found a "group mind" of certain groups of cells; and an "organ mind" of the various groups composing an organ of the body; and these in turn are grouped together in what we have called the Corporeal Mind, which is the great group mind of the cells of the entire body. Just how these cells co-ordinate and co-operate in this way is unknown to science, but there seems to exist a high form of telepathic communication between them, of which we get a hint in the psychology of human crowds, in which there is found a "contagion of thought" between the various members thereof.

The cells possess mind not only for their own ends, but also mind which combining with like mind in other cells acts for the ends of the groups of cells, and then the larger groups, and finally the complete group composing the body. The combination of the cell-groups into organ groups of cells is so complete and thorough that to all intents and purposes each organ of the body may be regarded as a living creature, having a mind of its own. This is no flight of imagination, but is a cold scientific fact of biological psychology. Each organ has its own mind and uses it in its activities. When that mind becomes impressed with erroneous ideas (if the term may be used in this connection) it begins to manifest abnormally; and, likewise, when it is restored by properly directed mental treatment it resumes its normal functioning. These are proved facts of Mental Therapeutics and experimental psychology as may be seen by reference to any late work on these subjects.

Professor Haeckel, the eminent scientist, who cannot be accused of any leaning toward metaphysical theories, he being a leading advocate of the "materialistic" school of philosophy, says in one of his works: "The 'tissue soul' is the higher psychological function which gives physiological individuality to the compound multicellular organism as a true 'cell commonwealth.' It controls all the separate 'cell souls' of the social cells—the mutually dependent 'citizens' which constitute the community. The human egg cell, as soon as it is fertilized, multiplies by division and forms a community, or colony of many social cells. These differentiate themselves, and by their specialization, by various modifications of these cells, the various tissues which compose the various organisms are developed. The developed many-celled organisms of man and of all higher animals resemble, therefore, a social civil community, the numerous single individuals of which, are, indeed developed in various ways, but which were originally only simple cells of one common structure."

To those to whom this collective mentality of the cells composing an organ of the body, or the greater combination composing the body itself, may seem unthinkable, we would suggest a study of the action of collective mentality in the various forms of life. For instance, observation reveals the fact that a great school of fish seem to move by a common impulse, as if under the action of a collective mind; the same phenomenon being noted in the case of flocks of birds, herds of larger animals, and even in crowds of men as we shall see presently. The actions of the bees in a hive show such a close co-ordination that the animating spirit moving them has been called "the spirit of the hive."

Students of human psychology have noted the characteristics of the psychology of human crowds, audiences, congregations, mobs, etc. It is a proved fact of psychology that the various individuals composing a crowd of persons think, say, and do things when in the crowd that would be foreign to them as separate individuals. There is a strange "contagion of thought" among the individuals of a crowd. Each individual in a crowd loses a certain degree of individuality, and acquires a greater degree of collective mentality; he becomes a member or part of the "collective mind" of the crowd; at the same time the crowd itself takes on a being of its own, which disappears when the crowd is dissolved.

Le Bon, the great psychological authority on this subject, in his work entitled "The Crowd," says: "The most careful observations seem to prove that an individual immerged for some length of time in a crowd in action soon finds himself in a special state, which most resembles a state of fascination in which the hypnotized individual finds himself. The conscious personality has entirely vanished, and will and discernment are lost. All feelings and thoughts are bent in the direction of the hypnotizer. An individual in a crowd is a grain of sand amid other grains of sand which the wind stirs up at will.''

All of the above leads us to the inevitable conclusion that the same general principle of ''collective mind'' manifests in the case of the various organs and parts of the body. Every fact of physiology seems to sustain this idea, and the idea itself is based upon the soundest foundations of biology and psychology. The liver has its collective mind; the heart likewise; the stomach likewise; the kidneys likewise; the nervous system likewise; and so until every great department of the body is included in the list. Each of these collective minds has its own peculiarities, characteristics, and qualities, as we shall see as we proceed. And, all combined in collective mental co-ordination, compose the entire body itself, with its Corporeal Mind.

But, it must be always remembered that the individual cells are the units of which the whole body is built up. All corporeal mind is, in its elemental form, merely cell mind. And so, at the last, all disease must originate in the cells, and all cures must be directed toward the cells —the cell minds of course being the soul and spirit of the activity of the cell.

The best therapeutic theory today holds that

all disease is a failure of the cells to function properly, i. e., to do their full work, to repair waste, and to eliminate waste matter. This improper functioning may be the fault of individual cells, or it may result from a failure of cellgroups (large or small) to co-operate properly, and to work in harmony and unison. Sometimes there is manifested an actual rebellion of the cells or cell-groups. These failures of the cells to do their appointed work properly results in either local or else general conditions of disease or ill-health. Naturally, it follows that the diseased condition may be cured only by restoring the cell activities to natural functioning.

Nature often performs this curative work by bringing pressure to bear on the mind in the cells or cell-groups, but sometimes the Corporeal Mind itself seems to become obsessed with the delusion of disease, and in such cases it must be restored to normal condition by means of treatment from outside. Here is where Mental Therapeutics performs its great work. By reaching the mind in the cells and in the cellgroups the abnormal condition is neutralized and destroyed, and the normal condition restored. Even in cases in which there exists a material or mechanical cause for the disorder, proper stimulation of the mind in the cells and organs sets up an increased resistive and combative power, and the forces are rallied and directed toward the removal of the existing obstacle.

So, you see, Mental Therapeutics is not necessarily bound up with metaphysical, philosophical, or theological theories. Instead, it is based upon the combined discoveries of biology, physiology, and comparative psychology. There is a biological and physiological basis of cure underlying the theory and practice of Mental Therapeutics which is too often lost sight of by the over-insistence, on the part of some of its advocates, upon the acceptance of the metaphysical theories, philosophical hypotheses, and theological dogmas which they have attached to the general subject of mental healing.

But the student should ever remember, that, no matter how far away he seems to get from the cell and its mind, the basis of the system is to be found in the presence of mind in the cells of which the human body is composed. By holding close to this fundamental idea, one never can go very far wrong; nor wander far away from the path of solid scientific fact. Otherwise, beware the quagmires and swamps which beset the road.

LESSON V

THE SYMPATHETIC NERVOUS SYSTEM

Nature, or the Power that is behind Nature, has built up an intricate system of nerves, nerve centers, and nerve connectives, by means of which the Corporeal Mind is able to perform the manifold and complex activities and functions of the body which is composed of cells and cell-groups as we have seen. The greater part of this work is performed by a part of the nervous system of which but comparatively few persons have ever heard, much less have become familiar with.

We are so in the habit of thinking of the Cerebro-Spinal Nervous System, when we speak of "the nervous system," that we ignore the existence of the great Sympathetic Nervous System which performs all of the unconscious, involuntary activities of the body, such as the action of the heart, stomach, liver, kidneys, etc.; and which also attends to the important processes of secretion, nutrition, elimination, excretion, reproduction, etc.

The term "sympathetic" was originally applied to this great system of nerves and nerve centers by reason of the fact that there is a reciprocal action of the different cell-groups and parts of the body, one with another, in an apparent "sympathy" with each other. A disturbance in one part of the body sets up a disturbance and activity in other parts. The whole body suffers in sympathy with an injured or diseased part or member. Thus, a wound will produce feverishness; stomach trouble or indigestion will produce headaches, etc., etc. The secretions of the body respond quickly in "sympathy" with conditions in other parts of the body.

The Sympathetic Nervous System consists of a great cable of nerves running from the base of the skull to the coccyx or end of the spinal column; but not within the spinal column itself, as is the case with the cerebro-spinal cable or spinal cord. These cables run on each side of the body by the side of the vertebrae; and bunch out into ganglia or nerve centers along their course. These cables are connected by branch lines with the spinal nerves, and with other nerves of the cerebro-spinal system; and are also connected with branches running to all of the organs of the body.

The Cerebro-Spinal Nervous System is concerned with our conscious activities; and all of our conscious motions and work is performed by means of it. The Sympathetic Nervous System, on the other hand, performs the **unconscious** and involuntary motions and functions. By means of this latter system our hearts beat, our lungs inspire and expire, the blood circulates, the stomach and intestines perform their work of digestion and assimilation, the liver and kidneys their important offices, the glands of the body secrete the important juices, and the entire reparative and nutritive work of the body is performed. The Sympathetic Nervous System, and the Corporeal Mind that animates and directs its activities, never sleep or rest—they are always at work; while the Conscious Mind and its Cerebro-Spinal System rest in sleep about one-third of its time.

An important feature of the Sympathetic Nervous System is its series of **ganglia,** or knots of gray nerve matter, which are scattered through the body, particularly along each side of the spine. Each ganglion is a complex center, having branches radiating in several directions. In several places these ganglia are grouped together in still more complex arrangement, called a plexus (plural "plexi"). The principal plexus is the well known "Solar Plexus," which some have called "The Abdominal Brain" by reason of its high power, and complex arrangement. This important plexus is situated in the upper part of the abdomen, almost directly back of the "pit of the stomach," it is the center from which emerge nerves extending in all directions. This great center is regarded as the Central Office, or headquarters of the Corporeal Mind.

The student should be able to grasp the fact that the Corporeal Mind is really the **animating spirit** of the sympathetic nervous system and the organs controlled by it. Consequently, he will be able to see that whatever affects the Corporeal Mind must reflect through the sympathetic nerves upon the entire body controlled by its power. The way to reach the organs of the body unquestionably is through the Corporeal

Mind, by means of its great chain of sympathetic nerves. This is the scientific explanation of the processes of mental healing.

In the case of the reparative work of the cells performed after a wound has been caused to the body, as related in a preceding lesson, it is the Corporeal Mind that directs and guides the energies of the cells, the orders being transmitted over the wires of the sympathetic nervous system. A general alarm is sent out, and all hands are called into service. And so it is in the case of all natural healing, which is often called the **vis medicatrix naturae** or natures healing force. For the Corporeal Mind is not only the great regulator and governor of the physical activities, but also **the great natural physician of the body.**

As an instance of the control of the Corporeal Mind over the body, we have an excellent example in the regulation of the circulation of the blood. The blood does not flow through the body in a regular, invariable manner, in response to purely mechanical laws, as so many believe. On the contrary, the Corporeal Mind regulates the flow in accordance with the circumstances of the moment. When necessary millions of tiny capillaries are closed or opened up, as the case may be, in order to increase or decrease the blood supply to certain parts. The blood supply of each organ is regulated by the needs of that organ at that time, as determined by the Corporeal Mind governing it. Even the rate of the pulsations of the heart are under the control of this Corporeal Mind, and varies according to circumstances.

Or again, the healing of a wound; the knitting together of a broken bone; the complex arrangements made necessary by the processes of gestation and childbirth; and thousands of other wonderful manifestations of unconscious mind in physical processes; all these are the work of the Corporeal Mind working with its sympathetic nervous system. When we speak of "Nature" doing this or that in the work of helping along the curative work, or vital processes, of the body, we are referring to this Corporeal Mind acting through its wonderful sympathetic nervous system.

The Corporeal Mind is animated by two very potent motives, namely (1) the motive of self-preservation; and (2) the motive of the reproduction of the species. All of its wonderful work is along these two lines; these are the only two laws of action that it recognizes. This is why it strives ever to preserve health in the body, and also why it exerts a sometimes overpowering influence in the matter of sex-attraction.

Much that we call "sickness" is really but the effect of the Corporeal Mind to throw out of the system morbid and injurious material which has gathered there; fever is often but the attempt of the Corporeal Mind to burn up this debris which it fails to get rid of otherwise. If it is unable to get rid of the cause of the trouble, it tries to adjust itself to the impaired conditions, and strives to balance the physical functions so as to

get the best possible **results** unable conditions. The Corpor·
working toward life and heal·
Sometimes it undertakes **her**·
perate methods, in order **to** ·
particularly dangerous **condi**·

The following quotations fr·
thorities show that this Corp··
the name of **vis medicatrix na**tur·
or "vital force," or **similar** ter·
by science as the real source ·
no matter by what method it ·
effect.

"By the term 'efforts of n··
certain curative or **restorative** ·
vita, implanted in every liv··
body, constantly operative for ··
vation, or health. This **instinct**·
repair the human organism **is** ·
the event of a severed **or lost** ·
for instance; for Nature, **unaid**··
fashion a stump equal **to** one ·
of an eminent surgeon. Natu··
be equally potent in **ordinary**·
individuals, even when sever··
rest in bed, under favorable hyg··
etc., and speedily get well with··
or medicine."

"The **vis medicatrix naturae** is
factor in the amelioration of dis·
be allowed fair play." "We ar·
acknowledge a power of natural
ent in the body—a similar stat·

SUGGESTION

Mental States. It is an ax-
... healing that a pleasurable
... tive to the cure of disease,
... dition tends to induce in
... al physiological action.
... potent causes of disease;
... erfulness are potent causes
... ealth. Therefore the prac-
... "cheer up," encourage,
... atient's feelings, as an im-
... treatment. The very
... th and Hope in itself tends
... feelings and emotions in
... helps along the effect of
... A skilful ...
... manages to ...
... of cheerful...
... healing sugges...
... suggestion...
... with a measur...
... rful and Hap...
... of nothing be...
... long this lin...
... tation of th...
... lifting ...
... be ...
... is peculiar...

get the best possible results under the unfavorable conditions. The Corporeal Mind is ever working toward life and health for its owner. Sometimes it undertakes heroic and even desperate methods, in order to combat and defeat particularly dangerous conditions.

The following quotations from eminent authorities show that this Corporeal Mind, under the name of **vis medicatrix naturae,** or "Nature," or "vital force," or similar terms, is recognized by science as the real source of cure of disease, no matter by what method it may be called into effect.

"By the term 'efforts of nature,' we mean a certain curative or restorative principle, or **vis vita,** implanted in every living or organized body, constantly operative for its repair, preservation, or health. This instinctive endeavor to repair the human organism is signally shown in the event of a severed or lost part, as a finger, for instance; for Nature, unaided, will repair and fashion a stump equal to one from the hands of an eminent surgeon. Nature, unaided, may be equally potent in ordinary illness. Many individuals, even when severely ill, remain at rest in bed, under favorable hygiene, regimen, etc., and speedily get well without a physician or medicine."

"The **vis medicatrix naturae** is a very potent factor in the amelioration of disease, if it only be allowed fair play." "We are compelled to acknowledge a power of natural recovery inherent in the body—a similar statement has been

made by writers on the principle of medicine in all ages." "Whatever other theories we may hold, we must recognize the **vis medicatrix naturae** in some shape or other." "A natural power of the prevention and repair of disorders and disease has as real and as active an existence within us as have the ordinary functions of the organs themselves." Hippocrates, the founder of the science of medicine, said: "Nature is the physician of diseases." Ambrose Pare had inscribed over the door of the great medical school, the Ecole de Medicine of Paris, these remarkable words: **"Je le ponsez et Dieu le guarit,"** which freely translated means: "I dressed the wound, and God healed it!"

A careful investigation shows that this much vaunted **vis medicatrix naturae,** the "Nature" of medical science, is really mental in its nature; and is identical with our conception of the Corporeal Mind. Mind is ever at work in the physical processes of nutrition, assimilation, elimination, reproduction, and the reparative processes of cure. The basis of all true healing is to be found in this Corporeal Mind, under .whatever name it may be called—this fact must ever be kept in mind.

The Corporeal Mind, however, sometimes lags in its work; or else it becomes sluggish and apathetic; or perhaps discouraged from some cause or other. In such cases it may be stimulated to action, and even guided and set to work in the proper direction by means of the proper incentive coming through the Conscious Mind,

get the best possible results under the unfavorable conditions. The Corporeal Mind is ever working toward life and health for its owner. Sometimes it undertakes heroic and even desperate methods, in order to combat and defeat particularly dangerous conditions.

The following quotations from eminent authorities show that this Corporeal Mind, under the name of **vis medicatrix naturae,** or "Nature," or "vital force," or similar terms, is recognized by science as the real source of cure of disease, no matter by what method it may be called into effect.

"By the term 'efforts of nature,' we mean a certain curative or restorative principle, or **vis vita,** implanted in every living or organized body, constantly operative for its repair, preservation, or health. This instinctive endeavor to repair the human organism is signally shown in the event of a severed or lost part, as a finger, for instance; for Nature, unaided, will repair and fashion a stump equal to one from the hands of an eminent surgeon. Nature, unaided, may be equally potent in ordinary illness. Many individuals, even when severely ill, remain at rest in bed, under favorable hygiene, regimen, etc., and speedily get well without a physician or medicine."

"The **vis medicatrix naturae** is a very potent factor in the amelioration of disease, if it only be allowed fair play." "We are compelled to acknowledge a power of natural recovery inherent in the body—a similar statement has been

made by writers on the principle of medicine in all ages." "Whatever other theories we may hold, we must recognize the **vis medicatrix naturae** in some shape or other." "A natural power of the prevention and repair of disorders and disease has as real and as active an existence within us as have the ordinary functions of the organs themselves." Hippocrates, the founder of the science of medicine, said: "Nature is the physician of diseases." Ambrose Pare had inscribed over the door of the great medical school, the Ecole de Medicine of Paris, these remarkable words: **"Je le ponsez et Dieu le guarit,"** which freely translated means: "I dressed the wound, and God healed it!"

A careful investigation shows that this much vaunted **vis medicatrix naturae,** the "Nature" of medical science, is really mental in its nature; and is identical with our conception of the Corporeal Mind. Mind is ever at work in the physical processes of nutrition, assimilation, elimination, reproduction, and the reparative processes of cure. The basis of all true healing is to be found in this Corporeal Mind, under .whatever name it may be called—this fact must ever be kept in mind.

The Corporeal Mind, however, sometimes lags in its work; or else it becomes sluggish and apathetic; or perhaps discouraged from some cause or other. In such cases it may be stimulated to action, and even guided and set to work in the proper direction by means of the proper incentive coming through the Conscious Mind,

45

get the best possible results under the unfavorable conditions. The Corporeal Mind is ever working toward life and health for its owner. Sometimes it undertakes heroic and even desperate methods, in order to combat and defeat particularly dangerous conditions.

The following quotations from eminent authorities show that this Corporeal Mind, under the name of **vis medicatrix naturae,** or "Nature," or "vital force," or similar terms, is recognized by science as the real source of cure of disease, no matter by what method it may be called into effect.

"By the term 'efforts of nature,' we mean a certain curative or restorative principle, or **vis vita,** implanted in every living or organized body, constantly operative for its repair, preservation, or health. This instinctive endeavor to repair the human organism is signally shown in the event of a severed or lost part, as a finger, for instance; for Nature, unaided, will repair and fashion a stump equal to one from the hands of an eminent surgeon. Nature, unaided, may be equally potent in ordinary illness. Many individuals, even when severely ill, remain at rest in bed, under favorable hygiene, regimen, etc., and speedily get well without a physician or medicine."

"The **vis medicatrix naturae** is a very potent factor in the amelioration of disease, if it only be allowed fair play." "We are compelled to acknowledge a power of natural recovery inherent in the body—a similar statement has been

made by writers on the principle of medicine in all ages." "Whatever other theories we may hold, we must recognize the **vis medicatrix naturae** in some shape or other." "A natural power of the prevention and repair of disorders and disease has as real and as active an existence within us as have the ordinary functions of the organs themselves." Hippocrates, the founder of the science of medicine, said: "Nature is the physician of diseases." Ambrose Pare had inscribed over the door of the great medical school, the Ecole de Medicine of Paris, these remarkable words: **"Je le ponsez et Dieu le guarit,"** which freely translated means: "I dressed the wound, and God healed it!"

A careful investigation shows that this much vaunted **vis medicatrix naturae,** the "Nature" of medical science, is really mental in its nature; and is identical with our conception of the Corporeal Mind. Mind is ever at work in the physical processes of nutrition, assimilation, elimination, reproduction, and the reparative processes of cure. The basis of all true healing is to be found in this Corporeal Mind, under whatever name it may be called—this fact must ever be kept in mind.

The Corporeal Mind, however, sometimes lags in its work; or else it becomes sluggish and apathetic; or perhaps discouraged from some cause or other. In such cases it may be stimulated to action, and even guided and set to work in the proper direction by means of the proper incentive coming through the Conscious Mind,

get the best possible results under the unfavorable conditions. The Corporeal Mind is ever working toward life and health for its owner. Sometimes it undertakes heroic and even desperate methods, in order to combat and defeat particularly dangerous conditions.

The following quotations from eminent authorities show that this Corporeal Mind, under the name of **vis medicatrix naturae,** or "Nature," or "vital force," or similar terms, is recognized by science as the real source of cure of disease, no matter by what method it may be called into effect.

"By the term 'efforts of nature,' we mean a certain curative or restorative principle, or **vis vita,** implanted in every living or organized body, constantly operative for its repair, preservation, or health. This instinctive endeavor to repair the human organism is signally shown in the event of a severed or lost part, as a finger, for instance; for Nature, unaided, will repair and fashion a stump equal to one from the hands of an eminent surgeon. Nature, unaided, may be equally potent in ordinary illness. Many individuals, even when severely ill, remain at rest in bed, under favorable hygiene, regimen, etc., and speedily get well without a physician or medicine."

"The **vis medicatrix naturae** is a very potent factor in the amelioration of disease, if it only be allowed fair play." "We are compelled to acknowledge a power of natural recovery inherent in the body—a similar statement has been

made by writers on the principle of medicine in all ages.'' ''Whatever other theories we may hold, we must recognize the **vis medicatrix naturae** in some shape or other.'' ''A natural power of the prevention and repair of disorders and disease has as real and as active an existence within us as have the ordinary functions of the organs themselves.'' Hippocrates, the founder of the science of medicine, said: ''Nature is the physician of diseases.'' Ambrose Pare had inscribed over the door of the great medical school, the Ecole de Medicine of Paris, these remarkable words: **''Je le ponsez et Dieu le guarit,''** which freely translated means: ''I dressed the wound, and God healed it!''

A careful investigation shows that this much vaunted **vis medicatrix naturae,** the ''Nature'' of medical science, is really mental in its nature; and is identical with our conception of the Corporeal Mind. Mind is ever at work in the physical processes of nutrition, assimilation, elimination, reproduction, and the reparative processes of cure. The basis of all true healing is to be found in this Corporeal Mind, under .whatever name it may be called—this fact must ever be kept in mind.

The Corporeal Mind, however, sometimes lags in its work; or else it becomes sluggish and apathetic; or perhaps discouraged from some cause or other. In such cases it may be stimulated to action, and even guided and set to work in the proper direction by means of the proper incentive coming through the Conscious Mind,

get the best possible results under the unfavorable conditions. The Corporeal Mind is ever working toward life and health for its owner. Sometimes it undertakes heroic and even desperate methods, in order to combat and defeat particularly dangerous conditions.

The following quotations from eminent authorities show that this Corporeal Mind, under the name of **vis medicatrix naturae,** or "Nature," or "vital force," or similar terms, is recognized by science as the real source of cure of disease, no matter by what method it may be called into effect.

"By the term 'efforts of nature,' we mean a certain curative or restorative principle, or **vis vita,** implanted in every living or organized body, constantly operative for its repair, preservation, or health. This instinctive endeavor to repair the human organism is signally shown in the event of a severed or lost part, as a finger, for instance; for Nature, unaided, will repair and fashion a stump equal to one from the hands of an eminent surgeon. Nature, unaided, may be equally potent in ordinary illness. Many individuals, even when severely ill, remain at rest in bed, under favorable hygiene, regimen, etc., and speedily get well without a physician or medicine."

"The **vis medicatrix naturae** is a very potent factor in the amelioration of disease, if it only be allowed fair play." "We are compelled to acknowledge a power of natural recovery inherent in the body—a similar statement has been

made by writers on the principle of medicine in all ages." "Whatever other theories we may hold, we must recognize the **vis medicatrix naturae** in some shape or other." "A natural power of the prevention and repair of disorders and disease has as real and as active an existence within us as have the ordinary functions of the organs themselves." Hippocrates, the founder of the science of medicine, said: "Nature is the physician of diseases." Ambrose Pare had inscribed over the door of the great medical school, the Ecole de Medicine of Paris, these remarkable words: **"Je le ponsez et Dieu le guarit,"** which freely translated means: "I dressed the wound, and God healed it!"

A careful investigation shows that this much vaunted **vis medicatrix naturae,** the "Nature" of medical science, is really mental in its nature; and is identical with our conception of the Corporeal Mind. Mind is ever at work in the physical processes of nutrition, assimilation, elimination, reproduction, and the reparative processes of cure. The basis of all true healing is to be found in this Corporeal Mind, under .whatever name it may be called—this fact must ever be kept in mind.

The Corporeal Mind, however, sometimes lags in its work; or else it becomes sluggish and apathetic; or perhaps discouraged from some cause or other. In such cases it may be stimulated to action, and even guided and set to work in the proper direction by means of the proper incentive coming through the Conscious Mind,

or else directed immediately to itself. This fact makes possible all forms of mental healing, no matter under what name they may operate, or under what theory they may proceed—the basic fact remains the same.

And, alas! the rule works both ways. For we find that much disease is caused, maintained, and perpetuated by means of wrongful suggestions or ideas implanted in the Corporeal Mind by means of influences, suggestion, teaching, advice or other methods of implanting an idea in the mind. The Corporeal Mind, though very set in its way as a rule, is affected by suggestion or wrong ideas if strongly and repeatedly presented to it. And when it finally is affected by these ideas, it manifests its false belief by means of its very efficient system of sympathetic nerves reaching to all parts of the body—and disease and improper functioning begins. Next to false ideas, perhaps, Fear is the most potent factor in this mental causation of disease. Fear paralyzes the activities of the Corporeal Mind, and prevents it from doing its work properly and efficiently.

It is to be hoped that the student will not pass over these important basic and fundamental explanations on the ground that they are "dry reading." Such a course would be very foolish, indeed; for it is necessary that these fundamental and basic principles of the theory of the cause and cure of disease may be thoroughly grasped and remembered, in order that the principles of healing may have an intelligent foundation.

LESSON VI

MENTAL CAUSES OF DISEASE

Before proceeding to the consideration of the subject of the healing of disease by the power of mind, it will be well for us to pause for a moment that we may realize the potency of the mind in the direction of causing disease. For, let us not try to escape this truth, mind turned in the wrong direction will as surely cause disease as mind turned in the right direction will cure disease. The mental motive power runs when reversed as well as when turned forward.

Medical science, in its history, has taken note of many instances of great mental epidemics, accompanied by physical ills, disease, and death. Fear is contagious, as all physicians know, and when it is based on a strong belief in a suggested idea of disease, the disease spreads with marvellous rapidity. The pages of the records of medical science are filled with the testimony of eminent physicians regarding this evil potency of mind in the direction of causing disease. The following are typical instances of this testimony:

"Diabetes from sudden mental shock is a true, pure type of a physical malady of mental origin."—**Sir Samuel Baker.**

"In many cases, I have seen reasons for believing that cancer had its origin in prolonged anxiety."—**Sir George Paget.**

47

"I have been surprised how often patients with primary cancer of the liver lay the cause of this ill-health to protracted grief or anxiety. The cases have been far too numerous to be accounted for as mere coincidences."—**Dr. Murchison.**

"Eruptions on the skin will follow excessive mental strain. In all these, and in cancer and epilepsy, there is a predisposition. It is remarkable how little the question of physical disease from mental influence has been studied."—**Dr. Richardson.**

"My experiments show that irascible, malevolent and depressing emotions generate in the system injurious compounds, some of which are extremely poisonous; also that agreeable, happy emotions generate chemical compounds of nutritious value, which stimulates the cells to manufacture energy."—**Prof. Elmer Gates.**

Dr. Hack Tuke, in his important work on the influence of the mind over the body, gives numerous cases of the causing of serious diseases by ideas held in the mind, or by simple mental states induced by fear. He gives many cases in which paralysis, jaundice, premature greyness and baldness, decay of the teeth, uterine troubles, erysipelas, eczema, and impetigo, have been caused in this way.

The records of physiological psychology contain many references to cases in which serious illness, and even death, have been caused by the efforts of practical jokers to "scare" their victims. The usual plan is to have several persons, during the course of a few hours, tell the victim that he is looking very ill, and that his appearance resembles that of another friend who grew suddenly ill and then died. The usual result is that the victim will become frightened, and in some cases be actually prostrated with weakness and compelled to take to his bed.

Medical students frequently contract the diseases whose symptoms they have been studying in their text-books. Moreover, it is an established fact that specialists in medical practice frequently contract the very disease that they have been studying so closely, and treating so continuously in their practice. The strong mental image tends to influence the Corporeal Mind, and that manifests in physical disorder. Many persons have contracted diseases described in detail in the patent medicine almanacs and other fear-producing printed matter describing the disease for which the medicine is intended.

Medical annals also contain numerous references to cases in which persons have died from the belief and fright arising from having taken what they have supposed to be poison, but which in reality was some harmless drug. Cases are known in which such patients died after having manifested all the symptoms of poisoning by the drug that they had supposed they had taken, but of which an autopsy failed to reveal even a trace.

MENTAL THERAPEUTICS

The well-authenticated instances of the production of **stigmata,** or the marks of the nails on the hands and feet of the crucified Savior, on the bodies of religious devotees who have too long contemplated the crucifix, is an instance of the power of the Corporeal Mind over the body which it controls. Suggestionists have producted blisters and even scars on the arms of patients, by suggesting that the harmless court-plaster placed on the arm was a strongly irritant chemical. Strong sympathy, accompanied by a vivid imagination, has caused persons to suffer the pain being undergone by others; in many cases even faint pink marks corresponding to the scars on the injured person have appeared on the body of the sympathetic relative or friend. It is a fact of common experience that many men suffer from sympathetic nausea during the pregnancy of their wives, and as many more experience soreness and pain around the lower part of the spine, accompanying the labor-pains of their wives during the birth of their children.

Hair has turned grey from emotion; milk has been rendered poisonous in the breasts of nursing mothers, from similar causes; it is frequent that nausea is produced by some story relating disgusting details, or even from the memory of a similar occasion; the thought of certain acid fruits, a lemon for instance, will cause the water to flow from the mouth; the bowels are frequently moved after one has thought of some unpleasant cathartic medicine one has taken at some time in the past; physicians know that menstruation in one woman frequently results in a similar happening in the case of other women around the first one who become aware of the fact, even though their regular monthly periods have not as yet arrived.

Carter quotes a case in which a lady saw three fingers cut from the hand of a child, in an accident. She was so affected that her hand began to pain her, and swelling resulted. The three fingers of her hand, corresponding to those cut from the hand of the child, became badly inflamed; an incision becoming necessary to evacuate the pus that had formed. Prof. James says: "The unconscious mind as revealed by hypnotism can exercise marvelous control over the nervous, vaso-motor, circulatory and other systems. There seems to be no reasonable grounds for doubting that, in certain chosen subjects, congestion, burns, blister, raised papules, bleeding from the nose or skin can be produced by suggestion." The significance of this lies in the fact that the hypnotic state is now recognized as one in which suggestion has an exaggerated effect; suggestion in the waking state, or even the auto-suggestion of the person himself, operates along the same lines, and sometimes in quite as marked a degree.

Dr. Schofield tells his students that the effect of a purgative pill has been rendered **nil,** and has been made to produce sleep under the belief that it was an opiate pill; and that, on the other hand, an opium pill given for sleep has failed to produce it, but acted as a strong purgative under the belief that it really was this; that great grief affects the entire body; and that he has known the breaking off of a marriage engagement to produce profound anaemia, or to whiten the hair within twenty-four hours.

As for the effect of "pure imagination" on the body, under the suggestion and belief in placebos, or other "make believe" remedies, such as bread-pills, etc., every physician can supply numerous evidences, if he feels so disposed, and thinks you are to be trusted. Bread-pills have cured many diseases, and have also produced strong purgative action when taken under the belief that they are extra strong purgative pills. Some physicians with a greater scientific curiosity than a regard for their patients have produced almost at will the entire range of physical conditions by prescribing harmless and inactive chemical substances accompanied with the strong suggestion of their effect. And, as every physician knows only too well, a hysterical patient will manage to counterfeit, and thus eventually to actually induce, a great range of physical disorders.

There is no need for extending this recital, for an entire book might be filled with instances of this kind. The one principle which is illustrated in all of these cases, and all like them, is this: That the Corporeal Mind which has control of the functions of the physical body, from great to small, simple to complex, is amenable to suggestion or insinuated ideas—either those of other persons, or those which are "picked up" by the conscious mind of the person himself. The suggestions or insinuated ideas, once accepted, tend to manifest it in action and outward expression, and thus cause to appear in physical form and conditions that which originally existed in the mind alone.

From this it is seen that the real cause of many cases and forms of physical disorders and disease is to be found in these suggested or acquired ideas or thoughts which have been accepted by the Corporeal Mind, and subsequently manifested into objective forms, states and conditions.

Consequently, the practitioner of Mental Therapeutics must always seek for these mental causes of the diseases which he is called upon to treat and heal. While, of course, he must direct his treatment to the physical conditions as they exist at the time of the treatment, he must also at the same time strive to reach and remove the original erroneous idea or thought which has really caused the whole trouble. In this way he discovers and removes the roots of the trouble, and does not content himself with merely treating and removing the consequences, effects, and results thereof—the symptoms, in short.

In Lesson II we have seen that the Subconscious Mind (of which the Corporeal Mind is a phase or aspect) will continue to harbor and manifest these erroneous ideas and thoughts until the following things happen, viz.: (a) The idea is neutralized, cancelled, and replaced by a sufficiently strong opposing idea or suggestion; or (b) the accepted suggested idea is traced back to its birth in the mind of the person, and is thereupon shown to be erroneous, based on wrong premises, and therefore untrue; in both of which methods the erroneous and harmful idea is wiped from the tablets of the mind, and ceases to exist—or to express it otherwise, the erroneous idea is painted over by the new and true idea, and ceases to appear in the mind, or to manifest in form and action.

This point of practice is worthy of special emphasis, and of careful thought and remembrance, for it goes right to the root of the trouble and eradicates the seed of the foul mental growth that is causing the trouble. Too often, the mental healer, like his brother, the medical doctor, contents himself with treating and removing the outward symptoms of the internal trouble. Try to discover the root of the trouble, and manage to kill it out at the same time you are remedying the manifestations arising from its presence in the mind of the patient. This, and this alone, is true and complete mental healing of disease.

LESSON VII

THE FUNDAMENTAL PRINCIPLE OF CURE

It is a fundamental principle of Mental Therapeutics that all forms of cures of diseases are really but different phases of mental cure. That is to say that in all healing processes the active principle is always found to be the mind in the cells, cell-groups, organs, or in the body as a whole. The **vis medicatrix naturae,** the healing powers of Nature, which performs all the curative work of the body, is mental in its elemental nature; therefore, all cures are mind cures, at the last.

The healing processes of the body are not blind forces, or mechanical energies, but, on the contrary, are characteristically mental in their activities. There is an intelligence at work in these processes; instinctive and subconscious though it may be, it still manifests all the characteristics of intelligence. There is always manifest the existence of a working plan and purpose, and an endeavor of the Corporeal Mind to accomplish the results indicated in such plan and purpose.

This may be seen more clearly when we stop to consider that each cell, and each group of cells, is a living, mental something, and not a mechanical, inert, lifeless thing moved only by external forces. The energies of the cell abide within the cell, and manifest in accordance with intelligent processes. The curative process always consists of the repairing of waste tissues, and in a harmonious readjustment of mutual relations and conditions by the activities of the cells themselves.

Even when external remedies and methods are used they are seen to be merely the supplying of the cells with proper stimuli, nourishment, and aid; or, perhaps, of removing mechanical or other obstacles from their way. The mind in the body, organs, and cells performs all the real curative work; all else is but an aid or help to the mental force latent within the body, organ, or cells.

The physician may administer a purgative, and this by removing undesirable and harmful substances from the system makes easier the task of the mind within the body. Or the surgeon may clean and drain the wound, thus taking a portion of the work from the cells, and rendering easier their other work. Or, the surgeon may place in juxtaposition the broken bones, and hold them into place by bandages, and then the mind in the cells does the healing work and knits them together. Man aids, but Nature cures—and Nature is mental in its final analysis.

More than this, medical science—at least the advanced and more intelligent teachers of it— recognize the fact that disease is not, as was formerly supposed, a foreign something that attacks the system. What is called "disease" is in very many cases but the symptoms of the efforts of Nature to eliminate objectionable and harmful conditions, and to resume normal states of functioning and activity. The theory of many thoughtful physicians is that disease is frequently really a self-preservative action on the part of Nature—an action by which she seeks to preserve the body by setting up conditions designed to combat abnormal conditions which have arisen. If Nature is unable to throw off the abnormal conditions, it at least accommodates itself to the new state of affairs, and strives to make the best of it—to manage to get the best possible results, or the least possible measure of harm.

This being recognized—and it cannot be denied—it follows that anything that will aid the mental action of the cells, organs, and body in this reparative work must aid the cure. And here is where Mental Therapeutics comes in. Nothing can aid and strengthen, direct and sustain, the mind in the cells, organs, and body better than Mind itself. Whatever strengthens the Corporeal Mind, and directs its energies effectively, must materially aid in the work of cure. And this is just what is accomplished by Mental Therapeutics. The Corporeal Mind, under the proper stimulus of Mind, will not only manifest latent powers and energies heretofore unmanifested, but will also obey the direction and guidance of a phase of mind more positive than itself, and thus act more efficiently. Upon this fundamental principle of practice all scientific mental healing is based.

MENTAL THERAPEUTICS

Sidney Murphy, M. D., an American authority, says of the reparative forces of Nature inherent in the organism: "It is a remedial effort, not necessarily successful, and an attempt to change, or have changed, existing conditions. Any improper relation of the living organism to external agents necessarily results in an injury to that organism, which by virtue of its being self-preservative immediately sets up defensive action, and begins as soon as possible to repair the damages that have accrued. This defensive or reparative action, of course, corresponds to the conditions to be corrected, and its persistence will depend upon the damages to be repaired, and the intensity and persistence of the causes that produced it. Serious injury present or impending will demand serious vital action; desperate conditions, desperate action. But in all cases the action is vital, an attempt at restoration, and the energy displayed will exactly correspond to the interests involved and the vitality that is available."

Another American authority, S. F. Meacham, M. D., says: "Disease is a failure of the cells to make good their waste, or to do their full duty. This may be an individual matter with the cell, or may result from imperfect co-operation; there may be a mutiny in the co-operative commonwealth constituting the body. * * * Any failure of this kind is disease either local or general, according to the importance of the mutinous or weakened cell. A cure results when the cells again do their work; or when other

58

cells learn to do that particular work, which is sometimes the case. A remedy is any substance, or force, or procedure that will stimulate, or help, or remove obstacles that prevent these cells from doing their work. Keep in mind that the life process acting through or in the cell does the work, whether aided or alone. * * * The process going on in each cell is an intelligent one, and all intrinsic methods are really but suggestions offered to the cell, the real worker; and the fact is that any one of these helps may be chosen, and all may be rejected.

"The repair of a cell is as equally an intellectual a process as any other can be. * * * The cell is not a mere machine, but a living entity, doing everything that the body does. It eats, drinks, moves, reproduces its kind, selects its foods, repairs its waste, etc. These are intellectual processes, but may not be conscious. * * * Cure consists in the repairing of wasted tissues, and in the cells restoring and repairing themselves into a definite pattern necessary to mutual work, so that the commonwealth may prosper. * * * The cells must build up the waste, and this they do by their internal forces; all disease is really cured by internal force, viz., force resident in the cell itself. Here we all stand around the suffering cell, one with drug-power in his hand, another with electricity, or water, or heat, or directed attention, thought-force, or more nourishment which necessitates a better circulation to that area, or some other of the thousand therapeutic measures, and we are close enough together at last to see that we are simply using different stimuli to try to aid the real worker within the cell to do his work, by furnishing not only material when that is necessary, but force as well, that out of the abundance his work may be easy and rapid.''

Dr. Thomson J. Hudson, the eminent American authority upon the subconscious processes of mind, says: ''Granted that there is an intelligence that controls the functions of the body in health, it follows that it is the same power or energy that fails in case of disease. Failing, it requires assistance; and that is what all therapeutic agencies aim to accomplish. No intelligent physician of any school claims to be able to do more than to 'assist nature' to restore the normal conditions of the body. That it is a mental energy that thus requires assistance, no one denies; for science teaches us that the whole body is made up of a confederation of intelligent entities, each of which performs its functions with an intelligence exactly adapted to the performance of its special duties as a member of the confederacy. There is, indeed, no life without mind, from the lowest unicellular organism up to man. It is therefore a mental energy that actuates every fibre of the body under all its conditions. That there is a central intelligence that controls each of these mind organisms, is self-evident. * * * It is sufficient for us to know that such an intelligence exists, and that, for the time being, it is the controlling energy that normally regulates the action of the myriad

FUNDAMENTAL PRINCIPLE OF CURE

cells of which the body is composed. It is, then, a mental organism that all therapeutic agencies are designed to energize, when, for any cause, it fails to perform its functions with reference to any part of the physical structure."

When this great principle of therapeutics—the principle that all cures are really performed through and by means of cell-activity; and that cell activity is mental, and under the control of the confederated minds of the totality of the cell-life of the body—is clearly perceived, then the great mystery of Mental Therapeutics vanishes. For when this principle is grasped, it is perceived that all cures are really mental cures, no matter by what methods or means the mental forces are called into operation. This being granted, it is seen that Mental Therapeutics is simply the calling into operation of the mental forces resident in the cells, organs, and entire physical system, but not by means of physical remedies or appliances, but rather by a direct appeal to the Corporeal Mind itself, and thus to the cell-minds and organ-minds.

Mental healing, in any of its forms and phases, is the most direct and immediate form of healing there is. Instead of proceeding in a roundabout way to get at the mind in the cells, organs, and parts, and thus to rouse it into activity, it makes a direct appeal to headquarters—the Corporeal Mind—and energies it into activity. The Corporeal Mind, which is very amenable to suggestion or instructions properly given it, falls in with the methods of cure stated to it by the

61

healer, or the person himself. It sends directing messages to the diseased organs and cells, and stimulates them to greater activity, if this is needed; or, again, it may recreate harmony where discord has been manifested. It proceeds to exercise its supreme co-ordinating power, and regulates and adjusts, directs and guides, the activities of the cells and organs.

As we proceed with our lessons we shall see that although mental healing has been practiced from time immemorial, under various names, forms, disguises, and based upon many theories of varying degrees of rationality, still the underlying principle has ever been one, and one only, i. e., that briefly outlined in this lesson and those which have preceded it. The effect of all of these varying methods and forms of mental treatment—plainly stated or else disguised under some fanciful theological or metaphysical theory—is identically the same, viz., the rousing into activity and operation of the mind in the cells and organs of the body, under the co-ordinating influence of the Corporeal.Mind. The student who understands this principle will ever find it present under and back of each and every instance of mental healing. The cures are not made by reason of the fanciful theories—but in spite of them. Remember this always!

LESSON VIII

THE HISTORY OF MENTAL THERAPEUTICS

The history of Mental Therapeutics is as old as the history of healing of any kind; for from the very beginning of the practice of healing there is found to have been practiced some of the manifold forms of mental healing. It is interesting to glance in passing at the history of the many phases and forms of mental healing of which the race has taken advantage.

Perhaps the earliest forms of mental healing were those connected with the magicians, medicine-men, or primitive priests of the savage tribes—from the very dawn of history mankind has taken unto itself priests, magicians, and medicine-men. And, just as naturally as the proverbial duck takes to water, so have these priests, magicians, and medicine-men taken to the healing of disease. This, perhaps, because the savage usually regards disease as something caused by the influence of devils, and evil influences, which must be chased away by the power of the magician or priest.

We, who can afford to smile at the superstition of these savages, must not make the mistake of supposing that these priests and magicians performed no cures. On the contrary, they did perform cures; and their prototypes among the savage tribes of this day are still performing cures, in the same way and for the same reason.

MENTAL THERAPEUTICS

Travelers relate instances of wonderful cures performed by these medicine-men, priests, or magicians in Africa, South America, and other portions of the world in which savages still dwell in remote regions.

The magic performances of these medicine-men or magicians are directed toward the chasing away of the demons of disease. They believe in the power of the demons; and they believe in the power of the magicians—else they would not employ their services. The expectant attention and the imagination of the sick persons is called into operation by the magic ceremonies. All students of modern Mental Therapeutics understand the potency of the aroused imagination and expectant attention of a patient—this mental attitude results in a very decided curative and reparative activity on the part of the mind in the cells and the organs. The savage has a great amount of vital power, or vital mind, in his body, owing to his natural methods of living; and this once directed toward the process of cure begins to show marked improvement. The patient, noting the improvement, is encouraged in his faith and belief, and the reparative force thus gains additional power; and so on until the cure is made.

The next step is that of healing by religious ceremonies, which is performed by the priests of the primitive peoples of history. The priests claiming to be chosen instruments of the Deity, naturally claimed the divine power of healing among other gifts. Their favorite method was to lay on hands, accompanied by certain ceremonies of their particular religion. The literature and monumental remains of ancient Egypt, Greece, Rome, Persia, India, and China shows that the laying-on-of-hands was a favorite and common method cure in those days and lands. There are evidences of it having been practiced nearly thirty-five hundred years ago in Egypt; it was also practiced extensively in ancient Chaldea and Persia several thousand years ago.

But this custom, so well established in the mind of the race, did not perish with the ancient religions. On the contrary, it has always been a feature of the Christian religion—in fact it formed one of the strong foundation stones of that religion, as of every other religion in its early days. Healing the sick and casting out devils were two of the special offices of the early disciples; and the priesthood naturally took over the privilege and practice when they replaced the early disciples.

In the Middle Ages healing by means of religious ceremonies, charms, and blessings was very common. Sacred relics, altars, shrines, and holy places were visited by great multitudes of persons, many of whom experienced cures of their physical ailments. This practice, in fact, has endured unto this day in many parts of Europe. All over certain countries of Europe are to be found the holy wells, and holy shrines, where miracles of healing are performed. The many crutches, and other tokens of former illness, which have been left at these holy places as a token of cure, establish the fact that the power has not departed from them—or, rather, that the power of the mind aroused by faith and expectant attention still operates in the direction of cure.

Later on, some of the kings and queens took over the gift of healing, probably much to the disgust of the priests whose revenues were thus affected. We find many records of "the King's Touch," or "the Royal Touch," in the Middle Ages, or afterward. There arose a belief that the touch of the hand of the monarch was a sure cure for scrofula and kindred disorders of the blood and skin. So at certain times of the year great multitudes would present themselves to the ruling monarch in order that they might be made whole by his healing touch.

Those who may be inclined to smile at the idea of the monarch having any special power to heal should study the records of the times. Thousands were healed in this way, if we are to believe the testimony of eminent persons then living, including many distinguished physicians of those times. For instance, Dr. Wiseman, an eminent surgeon of old-time London, says that he, personally, witnessed thousands of actual cures of this kind "without the assistance of medicine or surgery, and those, many of them, such as had tired out the endeavors of able surgeons before they came hither. * * * I must needs profess that which I write will little more than show the weakness of our ability when compared with his Majesty's, who cureth more in one year than all the surgeons of London have done in an age.''

The great successes of Franz Anton Mesmer in the latter part of the eighteenth century are now perceived to have arisen by reason of the power of faith and expectant attention, and not by any virtues of his theories of methods. He was followed by many who improved on his methods, and built upon his theories. Braid, an English physician, in 1841, dispelled the mystery of Mesmer's cures, by advancing a new theory— that of Hypnotism. For a time after this many physicians followed Braid's methods, and obtained great results. Then after a time came the school of the French hypnotists, who evolved the theory of "Suggestion," which asserted that the healing power arose not from the hypnotic methods, but rather from the "suggestion" or mental commands given in the hypnotic state. Then came others who discovered that Suggestion was equally efficacious when administered without any resort to hypnotism. This was the dawn of the modern scientific study of Mental Therapeutics—for it revealed the important fact that in mental states—particularly those of faith and expectant attention—there was to be found a great healing power.

The great modern interest in, and improvement in, the methods of Mental Therapeutics have arisen from the work of the practitioners of some of the many forms of "psychological healing," or "biological healing," so popular during the last half of the nineteenth century, all of which were offshoots of Mesmerism or Braidism. Gradually there sprung from this main trunk the several forms of Metaphysical Healing which became so popular the last quarter of the century last past, and which have grown so remarkably during the years of the present century.

The connecting link between the older schools of psychological healing, and the newer schools of metaphysical healing, is found in Dr. Phineas Parkhurst Quimby, a poor clockmaker of limited education, but of a quick mind and a strong personality, who lived in Maine, one of the New England States of America. Quimby was attracted to the teachings of Mesmerism about 1838, and soon developed into a successful mesmeric healer. He followed along the lines of John Bovee Dod's "Electro-Biology" for a time, but soon evolved a more metaphysical theory of his own. His new conception was that disease arose from erroneous thinking, and that cures may be performed by getting the patient to think rightly. Among his pupils were Dr. Warren F. Evans and Julius A. Dresser, both of whom afterward established what they called "The Mind Cure," which was the direct ancestor of the great "New Thought" movement now so popular in America and Europe. Another patient and pupil of Dr. Quimby's was Mary Baker Eddy, who afterward founded the great Christian Science movement, which now numbers its followers at a million or more—Christian

Science, however, now repudiates all descent from Quimby.

Springing up as a result of the success of the Mental Science, Christian Science, and New Thought movements, during the past twenty-five years, we find many instances of the desire of the people for religious and similar phases of mental healing. Divine healers by the score have appeared, flourished, and then disappeared. Francis Schlatter, the German shoemaker of Denver, Colorado, U. S. A., healed thousands of persons who flocked to his cottage, believing him to be a prophet of God. John Alexander Dowie, an English preacher, created great interest, first in Australia and then in Chicago, Illinois, U. S. A., by his many cures. He established a church in Chicago, the walls of which were lined with crutches, trusses, etc., of persons who had been healed by his prayers and laying-on-of-hands. Both Schlatter and Dowie have had many imitators, many of whom have met with more or less success.

The great New Thought movement, with its many divisions, and subdivisions, has a large following, and also has a great multitude of healers, all of whom make cures by the general methods of mental healing, though under many different theories and conceptions, and by many methods of application. Christian Science supports many fine churches and many healers and teachers, some of whom have grown wealthy as the result of their practice. The "Emmanuel Movement," started by some of the orthodox churches several years ago, is another illustration of the popularity of mental methods of healing—and also of the common desire of the public to have such healing given under the cover, and in the form of religious teachings.

The student must not, however, imagine for a moment that all of these modern schools and phases of mental healing admit that the basis and foundation of their cures are such as we have seen to exist, in the preceding lessons. On the contrary, they generally vigorously insist that their cures are made by reason of the truth of their particular theories and beliefs, or methods of treatment. They scout the idea of the simple, natural, scientific basis of mental cures, as taught in these lessons. They prefer the mystery—and the possible monopoly—of their own teachings.

But the cold-blooded scientific observer insists upon the fact of the simple, natural scientific basis and foundation, which always exists under the fanciful guises and forms. He sees that while each of the cults or schools has its own particular theory and teaching—each claiming that the other are lacking in truth; still each and every one of them are making cures, and in about the same proportion and percentage. Therefore, he claims that the truth lies not in any of their particular conceptions, but rather in a fundamental principle underlying them all, and common to all of their methods. This fundamental principle is that which forms the basis of these lessons; it is over and above any

cult or school—it is based upon scientific observation and logical thought, and not upon revela-
tion, inspiration, or religious dogma, or upon
metaphysical subtleties and hair-splitting.

LESSON IX

DISGUISED MENTAL HEALING

As the student has doubtless already surmised, there are many cures wrought by the underlying principle of Mental Therapeutics which, however, are not attributed thereto, but which are placed to the credit of some other healing agency or power, method or principle.

This must be so from the very nature of the fundamental principle of mental cures. It being seen that all healing really is performed by the mind in the cells, organs, and parts of the body; and that this mind is under the control of the Corporeal Mind; and that the latter takes up, accepts, and acts upon the suggestions reaching it from the minds of others; then it follows that mental cures may be made by agencies and methods which are accepted as efficacious by the Corporeal Mind, or rather by the great subconscious mentality of which the Corporeal Mind is a phase or part.

In accordance with this principle of operation, wonderful cures have been wrought by the most ridiculous and absurd methods and agencies, providing always that the method of agency was accepted as efficacious by the subconscious mentality of the person. The belief in, and faith in, almost anything under the sun (or over the sun) will act as a curative force along the lines above indicated. This being so, we naturally look for striking instances and examples of this natural law—and we find them on all sides. The history of medicine is filled with instances and examples of this kind, many of which are very amusing when one views them in the light of the scientific principle involved.

It has been known to physicians for many centuries that the "imagination" of the patient, if sufficiently aroused, was capable of working many important cures of serious ailments, not to speak of the less important ones. Physicians for centuries have laughed over this well-known fact, but without understanding the principle involved and called into effect. It is only during the past' twenty years or so that the medical profession has recognized the underlying psychology of cures by "imagination"; and even so, but a small number of physicians have had the keenness of perception, and soundness of judgment, to put into practice the principle which has been revealed to them by the great minds in the profession who have discovered the efficacy of such methods from actual practice.

It has long been the practice of physicians to administer "placebos" (i. e., "make believe" medicine) in the practice, when in doubt regarding the proper thing to prescribe. Colored water, strong-tasted drops, sugar-of-milk powders, bread-pills, and similar placebos have had their place in the list of remedies of most physicians. Originally intended to quiet the mind of the patient, and to satisfy the demands of the friends and family of the sick person for "some medicine," these placebos have justified their existence and employment. But it is a dull physician who does not soon discover that these placebos actually cause improvement and cures in many cases. The experience of any old physician (if he is foolish enough to relate it to a layman) will more than justify all that we have said of the virtue of placebos.

So true is it that the placebo has a decided therapeutic action, depending of course upon the particular belief aroused in the mind of the patient when it is prescribed, that many careful practitioners have not hesitated to say that many of the drugs on their list have no other virtue than that acquired in this way. Moreover, this principle is held to explain the fact that some practitioners have obtained wonderful results from certain remedies, or combinations of remedies, which their brethren failed to obtain after their attention had been called to them. The discoverer of a new remedy is filled with an earnest belief in it, which belief he communicates to his patient—can you doubt the result. The other physicians, lacking this faith, fail to impress it upon their patients—hence the less satisfactory result. An understanding of this principle has solved many a mystery of this kind—physicians are just beginning to understand the cause of the trouble.

Dr. Hack Tuke, an English physician of the last century, made a careful study of this interesting phase of mental healing; his book on the subject is still well worth reading and study, in spite of the recent discoveries of the underlying principle which the good doctor failed to discover. His book is filled with very interesting cases of cures by "imagination" (so he called it), but which we now recognize as genuine mental healing in disguise.

Tuke relates that he cured many cases of chronic rheumatism by rubbing them with a certain substance, without virtue in itself but for which he asserted magical and miraculous powers. To assure himself that this substance was without any real virtue in itself the good doctor changed it from time to time, sometimes using metal, then again wood, and sometimes wax or similar substances—the result was precisely the same in each case, the virtue being solely in the faith and belief inspired in the patient by his assertions. He relates that he cured warts in the same way; this result is accomplished by many persons who "pow wow" warts away from the bodies of their friends.

Tuke also mentions the interesting case of an army officer who was subject to severe cramps in the stomach, which powerful remedies failed to cure. Tuke finally gave him "a powder containing four grains of ground biscuit," which was to be administered every seven minutes, the greatest anxiety being expressed (within the hearing of the patient, of course) lest too much should be given—it being spoken of as a rare drug of great power. Tuke cured his man in a short time, the powerful drug (?) manifesting its wonderful virtues. Tuke also relates a case in which the house surgeon in a French hospital experimented with one hundred persons, prescribing sugared water for them; he then, with a great show of anxiety and concern, announced that he had given them a powerful emetic instead of the intended remedy. Tuke adds: "The result may easily be anticipated by those who can estimate the power of the imagination; no fewer than eighty—four-fifths of the entire number—were unmistakably sick."

An eminent physician recorded an instance in which a patient reported that he felt a decided improvement immediately after a clinical thermometer had been placed in his mouth—he thought that it was some new kind of therapeutic instrument. The physician, being wise beyond his times, continued the treatment and healed the man speedily. Similar experiences are furnished by the resident physicians in many hospitals where a large number of patients are admitted.

Schofield, in his interesting work upon the Unconscious Mind, relates a number of cases in which cures were performed by disguised mental healing. He also relates a number of cases in which the same principle has been incidentally called into operation without any intent to do so on the part of the physician. For instance, he relates that in the early days of Koch's tuberculin many patients rushed to Berlin to be treated. It was observed by the physicians administering the remedy that a certain set of symptoms (among others a rise of temperature after so many hours) usually followed the injection; these symptoms were accepted at first as being diagnostic of the existence of tuberculosis. But some of the physicians who knew something of the power of suggestion, made some tests— and obtained startling results. It was found that the patients usually anxiously awaited the occurrence of these particular symptoms, of which they had been informed by their fellow-patients. And, the tests proved that these same symptoms were manifested by many of the patients after they had been injected with pure water, without a trace of tuberculin.

Ferassi relates that he cured many cases of ague by giving the patient a charm consisting merely of the word "Febrifuge" written on it. Fever and ague, chills and fever, and similar complaints have been successfully treated by certain old women and old men in the neighborhoods affected, the method consisting merely of some sort of "pow wow," or mock "magic" treatment in which both the healer and the patient firmly believed. Seasickness, and carsickness, has yielded to some remedies of the nature of the placebo. Stewards on ocean liners furnish interesting testimony along these lines —though they are careful to whom they give their confidence, for obvious reasons.

Schofield relates many interesting cases of this kind. In one case he cured a woman brought to a London hospital as suffering from incurable paralysis of the spine for two years; she had spent all her money in treatments, without results, and was brought to the hospital pending her admission to a charitable home for incurables. Schofield cured her in two hours—he does not state his method, but says positively that there were "agencies which owed all their virtue to their influence on the mind." He also relates another case in which a paralyzed girl was cured when she learned that she had won the affections of the curate who used to visit her bedside. Another case of the same kind was cured at the Hotel Dieu, in Paris, solely by being impressed by the wonderful place, its noted doctors, and its wonderful reputation. Schofield says of this last case: "The good doctor just passed around, but had not time to treat her till the third day; by which time when he came around she was out of bed, walking around the room, quite restored by the glimpses she had got of his majestic presence."

The undoubted cures wrought by "patent medicines" composed of simple herbs and diluted alcohol, or even still more simple materials, are to be accounted for in the same way. The same is true of the wonderful "appliances," "electric garments," "rheumatic rings," and similar articles which are advertised so extensively from time to time—they all work cures, and obtain testimonials from grateful patients. The "tractors" of Elijah Perkins, the New England blacksmith, in the early part of the last century is another instance of the same principle. Perkins built metallic tongs which he called "tractors," with which he stroked the bodies of patients. He made great cures, and his fame extended all over the country, and even to Europe. His followers were numbered by the thousands. Finally the bubble was pricked by a physician who made a counterfeit pair of tractors of wood painted to resemble the metal of the genuine tongs—they worked just as well, and thereby **proved** the mental nature of the cures.

The student and practitioner of Mental Therapeutics should become familiar with this class of mental cures—cases in which the cure is attributed to some material remedy, appliance, or method, although really resulting from the mental principle called into operation. When the principle is once thoroughly understood, then one has the key to the whole class of strange cures. This knowledge prevents one from being led into error, and being persuaded to "follow after strange gods" in healing; it also enables one to avail himself of fanciful methods and forms, when he sees that the patient expects and demands the same. Such a course is not to be recommended as a regular thing—but there arise cases in which the healer must take the material as he finds it, and then work it into the proper shape by methods along the lines of the least mental resistance. But he must never lose sight of the true principle involved in the cure.

LESSON X

THREE METHODS OF MENTAL HEALING

While there are countless methods and processes of manifesting Mental Healing under the general principles of Mental Therapeutics, still these methods may be grouped into three general classes or principles of application. The student who will thoroughly acquaint himself with the underlying principle of each of these three general classes will be master of the entire system, for all methods or forms of application are found to be but some variation of one of these general classes, or else a combination of one or more of them.

These three general classes of the methods of applying Mental Healing are as follows: (1) Healing by Mental Suggestion; (2) Healing by Present Thought Induction; and (3) Healing by Distant Thought Induction.

The student should always remember, however, that it is a very rare occurrence indeed for any one of the above stated general methods to be employed exclusively. In most cases there is always a greater or less degree of combination or blending of two or more methods.

This last statement may be verified by analyzing the cases in which some one of the above stated methods is apparently exclusively employed. It will be found that (sometimes almost unconsciously) the principles of one or more of the other methods is blended with that which is specially employed. For instance, the practitioner using the method of Mental Suggestion almost always also uses Personal Thought Induction in the presence of the patient, and often also Distant Thought Induction when thinking of "the case" between treatments. In the same way, the practitioner employing the methods of Direct Thought Induction always invariably uses more or less Mental Suggestion (though he may do so unconsciously) when he is talking to the patient; and he also uses Distant Thought Induction when thinking of "the case" between treatments. And, in the same way, the practitioner employing the methods of Distant Thought Induction almost invariably uses Mental Suggestion when conversing with the patient regarding the arrangements for treatments, or in the correspondence concerning the same, and at the same time employs Personal Thought Induction when in the presence of the patient.

But, inasmuch as all of these methods proceed to effect cures by means of the same fundamental principle, i. e., **that of arousing into renewed and normal activity and functioning the mind in the cells, organs and part of the body of the patient,** the question of just what particular method, or combination of methods is used, is one of merely academic interest to the practitioner, and is to be subordinated to the question of "just how" to reach the mind of the affected parts.

The student and practitioner, however, will soon discover that some particular form of treatment is best adapted to the requirements of certain patients, while another form will best suit those of other patients, and so on. By understanding the fundamental sameness underlying the superficial differences in the three methods (and the variation thereof), and by acquainting himself with the best ways of applying each and all of these methods, the practitioner will be equipped to handle effectively any kind of case that presents itself for treatment, and to adapt his treatment to meet the personal idiosyncrasies or peculiarities of each patient.

The practitioner who allows himself to fall into the error of believing that some one particular method or principle of Mental Healing is the "whole thing," and the only thing, is placed at a disadvantage for obvious reasons. The broad-gauge practitioner is able to apply the principles of Mental Healing in a scientific manner, rather than in the spirit of partisanship, or narrow loyalty to some particular teacher or school. The best practitioner of Mental Therapeutics is he who "takes his own wherever he finds it," and presses it into service in his work—the true "eclectic" who takes what is best in many systems; who wisely selects and boldly employs. There is no place for narrowness and one-sidedness in Mental Therapeutics, if one wishes to become and remain a successful practitioner thereof.

While we shall, of course, explain the principles underlying each one of these three general classes of the methods of applying Mental Healing when we come to consider each in its proper place in these lessons, it will be as well for us to consider at this place the fundamental features and characteristics of each in turn, that we may form a clear mental conception of each, and perceive its place in the general system or principle of Mental Therapeutics.

(1) Mental Suggestion. By Mental Suggestion is not meant hypnotic suggestion, although in the public mind the two usually are regarded as the same. Hypnotic Suggestion is merely Mental Suggestion administered when the patient or subject is in the hypnotic state. As eminent authorities have well stated it, "the hypnotic condition is a state in which Mental Suggestion has an exaggerated effect;" but it should be thoroughly understood that Mental Suggestion does not depend upon the presence of the hypnotic state. The best practitioners of Mental Suggestion today do not seek to induce the hypnotic condition in their patients, and, in fact, in most cases they frown upon the practice of doing so.

The principle of Mental Suggestion is simply that of placing in the subconscious mind of the patient a firm, strong, positive idea of the physical condition sought to be induced in him. Suggestion differs from logical argument or reasoning inasmuch as it does not seek to convince by logical proof, but rather depends upon its acceptance by reason of **its strong insistence, and authoritative form of presentation.** The principle underlying Suggestion is indicated by the original meaning of the Latin terms from which it was derived, i. e., "suggero," meaning, literally, "to carry or place **under**." The technical meaning of "to suggest" is "to indirectly introduce into the mind."

Hollander cleverly defines Suggestion as: "a process of communication of an idea to the subconscious mind in an unobtrusive manner, carrying conviction; when consciously there is no inclination for its acceptance, and logically there are no adequate grounds for its acceptance." Bechterew, equally cleverly says: "Suggestion enters into the understanding by the back stairs, while logical persuasion knocks at the front door."

Mental Suggestion in Mental Healing conveys to the mind of the patient the idea or mental picture of the physical condition sought to be induced—**and it conveys this by words, spoken, written, or printed.** The subconscious mind accepting the idea or picture so introduced passes it on to that phase of itself known to us as the Corporeal Mind, and this in turn passes it on to the organ and cell minds concerned with that portion of the body in which the physical condition is sought to be induced or created.

This is the one point to be remembered regarding Mental Suggestion, at least at this stage of our lessons, viz.: **Mental Suggestion creates the desired idea in the Corporeal Mind by means of words—spoken, written, or printed.**

(2) Personal Thought Induction. By Personal Thought Induction the idea of the physical condition sought to be induced is introduced into the subconscious mind, and thus to the Corporeal Mind, and to the cells and organs governed by the latter—**but not by words, spoken, written, or printed,** as in the case of Mental Suggestion. There is a broad distinction here which the student should note and remember.

Personal Thought Induction, however, is always manifested when the practitioner is in the immediate personal presence of the patient—just as in the case of Mental Suggestion by words spoken. The principle involved is one of which we shall of course speak in detail, and in full, at the appropriate time in these lessons. For the present, however, it is sufficient to state that it is a fact known to students of advanced psychology that Thought, like magnetism or electricity, radiates from the thinker, and, coming in contact with the mental aura of the patient, tends to induce there a corresponding idea, thought, or mental picture of the physical condition which is sought to be induced in the patient.

These thought-vibrations, however, are not consciously perceived by the patient; instead, they are taken up only by his subconscious mind, and then passed on to the Corporeal Mind, and then to the cell and organ minds of his body. Once reaching the subconscious mind, the process is identical with the process manifested in cases of Mental Suggestion as above described. So you see the practical distinction between the two methods of Mental Healing so far considered, viz., Mental Suggestion and Personal Thought Induction, respectively, is simply that of **the difference in reaching the subconscious mind of the patient.** From that point and stage, the two processes are practically identical.

(3) Distant Thought Induction. In Distant Thought Induction we have the principle of Thought Induction, just described, **plus the manifestation of certain mental powers which serve to carry the thought-vibrations beyond the ordinary limits and range of Thought Induction.** In this form of Thought Induction the principle of Thought Radiation is extended so as to become available even though many miles separate the practitioner from the patient. It accomplishes for Thought Radiation that which the telescope accomplishes for the faculty of sight; or the telephone for the faculties of hearing and speech.

In Distant Thought Induction the practitioner (a) first creates in himself the mental idea and picture of the physical condition sought to be induced in the patient, just as in the case of Personal Thought Induction; then (b) he puts into operation certain powers of the mind and will (hereafter to be described and explained to the student) which serve to carry his thought vibrations to a distance—to project them into space, so as to reach the distant patient; then

(c) the vibrations reaching the subconscious mind of the patient are taken up, translated into ideas and pictures corresponding to those in the mind of the practitioner, and then passed on the Corporeal Mind, and thus to the cell-minds and organ-minds.

Summary. So, the student perceives, the underlying principle of each and every one of these methods of manifesting Mental Healing is the same, namely that of reaching the cell-minds, and organ-minds, of the patient, via the subconscious mind and the Corporeal Mind of the patient; and by producing or inducing in these mental planes of the patient the idea and mental picture of the physical conditions sought to be created, produced, or induced in him. This is the great, broad, general, underlying principle of Mental Healing—the rest is but the matter of application, technique, and good judgment in selecting the particular methods best adapted to the particular case. As we proceed, the student should frequently refer to the present lesson, so as to keep fresh and clear in his mind this important fundamental and basic fact of his treatments.

LESSON XI

MENTAL SUGGESTION

The principle of Mental Suggestion is based upon the fundamental fact that the mind of all human beings manifests a far greater range of activities on the subconscious plane than on the conscious plane; that nearly eighty-five per cent of its activities are on the subconscious plane; and that **the subconscious plane of the human mind is highly receptive and amenable to Suggestion.**

As explained in the preceding lesson, Mental Suggestion does not depend upon logical processes or argumentive proof for its efficacy; but rather bases its force and efficacy upon its positive appeal to the subconscious mind. The subconscious mind is by its very nature very receptive to suggestion; in fact, it may be said to instinctively accept any suggestion given it, unless the suggestion runs counter to some suggestion already accepted by it; or unless the conscious mind has positively forbidden the acceptance of the suggestion.

The conscious guardian of the threshold of the mind once relaxing his watchfulness, there is nothing to interfere with the acceptance of a suggestion by the subconscious mind, providing that the suggestions already accepted by it do not prevent the introduction of new and opposing ones. And, even in the last mentioned event, the old accepted suggestions may be neutralized by a constant flow of new suggestions of an opposite nature—the process having been aptly compared to the flowing of clear water into a bowl of dirty water, in which case the overflow gradually carries off the diluted dirty water, until finally the bowl is filled with perfectly clear water. This, in fact, is precisely what happens in most cases of Mental Healing by Mental Suggestion—the old, negative suggestions are first diluted and then carried off, being replaced by the new and positive ones.

It must be always remembered, however, that the words of a Mental Suggestion have no magic power in themselves; their only virtue consists in the fact that they represent ideas, which ideas are called into being in the mind by the hearing or reading of the words. Another point to be remembered is that Mental Suggestion is effective in proportion to the degree of feeling it arouses in the person to whom it is addressed. The reason of this last mentioned fact is that feeling always energies an idea in the mind, and makes it active and operative. The suggested idea or mental picture of a physical condition greatly desired by the patient is many times more active and effective than a suggested idea or mental picture of a condition which fails to arouse such feeling or desire.

Hollander well says regarding this point: "Suggestions convey ideas, and ideas are symbols of something thought or felt. The majority of ideas held in the mind of the race arise from feeling. People may not understand things, but they have experienced feelings or emotions regarding them, and have consequently formed many ideas therefrom. They do not always know the reason why an idea is held by them; they know only that they feel it that way. And the majority of people are swayed and moved, and act by reasons of induced feelings, rather than by the result of reasoning. When suggestion acts through the association of ideas, it is based upon the acquired impressions of the race, by which certain words, actions, manners, tones, and appearances are associated with certain previously experienced feelings. It is true that suggestions may accompany an appeal to the reason or judgment of the person influenced, and, indeed, are generally so used; but, strictly speaking, they constitute an appeal to a part of the mind entirely removed from reasoning and judgment. They are emotional, first, last, and all the time. Many personal appeals which are apparently made to reason are really made to the emotional side. One may subtly insinuate into an argument or conversation an appeal to the feelings or emotions of the hearer by an ideal indirectly conveyed. Such an idea will be 'felt' by the listener, who will accept it into his mind, and before long he will regard it as one of his own thoughts—he will make it his own. He will think that he 'thought' it, whereas, really, he simply 'feels' it, and the feeling is induced.''

The principle of many instances of effective Mental Suggestion is cleverly expressed in the epigram attributed to Aaron Burr, that eccentric and meteoric American statesman and political adventurer of genius, which runs as follows: "Truth is that which is boldly asserted, and plausibly maintained." The experienced practitioner of Mental Suggestion will at once recognize the aptness of this epigram as applied to the principle of suggestion. For, in the first place, he will recognize the fact that the power of a suggestion depends greatly upon the boldness, positiveness, and air of authority with which it is expressed. He will likewise recognize the fact that its effect will be greatly heightened by the introduction of some **plausible statement—having the color of logical argument or proof,** which serves to back up and sustain the statement boldly expressed in the suggestion.

But the experienced suggestionist has also learned the danger of attempting to logically prove by elaborate argument the statements of his suggestion. He knows that when he has been foolish enough to follow this course, the attention of the patient has been taken off the statement of the suggestion, and that therefore the suggestion loses its effect. He realizes the truth of the principle previously enunciated, i. e., that suggestion enters the back door of the mind, while reason and logic enters the front door—suggestion is not based upon logic or reason, though it may well be colored a little by plausible reasoning along general lines. When a suggestion awakens desirable feelings, emotions, or pictures in the mind of the patient, then the patient requires but a color of proof or reasoning to satisfy his mind; as has well been said "persons generally want **excuses** for their feelings, not reasons or logical proof." **They want to believe that which appeals to their desires and feelings,** and therefore a mere color of general plausible "reason" satisfies them fully, while an elaborate attempt at logical proof distracts their attention and causes the statement of the suggestion to lose its effect.

It is for this reason that Mental Suggestion is so powerfully operative in cases of Mental Healing. The mind of the patient is filled with the desire to be cured—to have health restored. This being the case, the entire emotional nature is strongly alive to suggestions of cure—there is no opposition to suggestions of cure and health, but rather is there an eagerness to accept any plausible reason or explanation of the way in which the cure is to be effected. The emotional nature is willing and eager to co-operate with the statement of health and cure, rather than to oppose it. When to this is added the strong mental command, bold statement, and authoritative utterance of the suggestion properly made, we have a most effective and efficient piece of mental machinery set into operation and motion.

There are three strong mental factors operating in the case of Mental Suggestion properly applied, which the student of Mental Healing should carefully note and remember. These **three** mental factors are as follows: (1) Earnest

Attention; (2) Expectant Attention; and (3) Pleasurable Mental States. Let us then consider each of these, briefly, in turn; for their importance must not be overlooked.

(1) Earnest Attention. It is a fact conceded by all students of the psychology of suggestion, that the effect of any suggestion depends materially upon the degree of attention given to it. This, of course, arises from the well-known psychological principle that the degree of perceptive impression of a sensation, the degree of its retention in the subconscious memory, and the degree of ease of its subsequent recollection, depend upon the degree of attention given it. Attention has been compared to the focus of a telescope or microscope. The strength of all mental impressions depend upon the degree of attention given at the time of their reception. The reason of the strength of certain impressions upon our minds is that earnest and concentrated attention was manifested at the time the impressions were received. If we give no attention at all to an object or happening in the world outside of our mind, then we receive no impression at all regarding it. This is one of the fundamental facts of psychology, remember.

Well, then, the patient coming to the Mental Healer for treatment is filled with interest and curiosity regarding the healer and his methods— the patient is like a child visiting a new scene of interest, a moving picture performance, for instance; his mind is open to even the slightest impression, and he is really in a mental state most favorable to suggestion. In fact, he is in a condition in which suggestion has an exaggerated effect. Hence the importance of the practitioner creating a strong initial impression, by his manner, demeanor, and words—before, during, and after the suggestive treatment. The ideal suggestive condition is here, remember.

(2) Expectant Attention. Practical psychologists recognize the value of the mental state known as Expectant Attention; it is an established fact that the expectancy, or earnest hope, of an improvement in the physical condition will act powerfully in the direction of inducing the desired condition. This is the secret of the power of Faith and Hope in all Mental Healing —the secret of the cures of the Faith Healers and religious healing cults. But, it may be argued, the average patient has not much faith and hope when he visits a Mental Healer for the first time. This is a mistake, for unless there had existed a certain amount of faith and hope in the mind of the patient, he would not have visited the practitioner at all. Though he may say that he has no hope or faith in the treatment, the very fact that he considers such treatment, visits the practitioner, **and pays his fee for treatment,** is a proof that faith and hope abide within his mind. The spark is there, and it is for the practitioner to blow it into a flame; for it is a mental state which acts powerfully in the direction of a cure.

(3) Pleasurable Mental States. It is an axiom of psychological healing that a pleasurable mental state is conductive to the cure of disease, while the reverse condition tends to induce imperfect and abnormal physiological action. Worry and Fear are potent causes of disease; Fearlessness and Cheerfulness are potent causes of cure and restored health. Therefore the practitioner should always "cheer up," encourage, and "brace up" the patient's feelings, as an important part of the treatment. The very encouragement of Faith and Hope in itself tends to produce pleasurable feelings and emotions in the patient, and thus helps along the effect of the suggestive treatment. A skilful practitioner of Mental Suggestion manages to "work in" many little suggestions of cheerfulness and happiness along with his healing suggestions. A prominent American suggestionist was wont to dismiss his patients with a strong suggestion of "You are Bright, Cheerful, and Happy—Strong and Well!" I know of nothing better to offer as a general pattern along this line than these words. The very repetition of them to oneself tends to induce an uplifting emotion and feeling—then what must be their effect upon a patient whose mind is peculiarly receptive to suggestion?

LESSON XII

PRINCIPLES OF SUGGESTION

There are certain leading principles connected with the effective use of Mental Suggestion, which should be carefully studied by the practitioner of Mental Healing, or the person who wishes to fit himself for such practice. These principles are not concerned with the nature of Mental Suggestion itself, but rather with the **application thereof,** particularly in the work of Mental Healing. I shall direct your attention to each of these principles in turn, and I ask that you carefully make note of the spirit underlying each.

Authority. The principle of Authority is an important one in the application of Mental Suggestion. It is based upon the well-established psychological law that the mind of the average person is strongly impressed by statements, spoken or written, which are expressed with the air of strong authority. It makes little or no difference whether the authority is real, or whether it is assumed, just so long as the air carries with it the assumption and implicit assertion of authority. This fact is well known to many students of human nature, especially to those whose success depends upon the acceptance of their statements or suggestions to the public.

It seems that the tacit assertion of authority

on the part of some one posing as a leader of thought, or practitioner of law, medicine, or theology, robs the average listener of his desire to analyze, weigh, consider, and demand proof of the assertions made to him. In the same way, there are found many persons who will question statements made to them in conversation, whereas they accept without question the same kind of statements made from the pulpit, or printed in the pages of a book. There seems to be some power in the printed word, or word spoken from the pulpit or judge's bench, to render unnecessary the production of proof of the truth of the word. The proof is taken for granted in such cases, it seems.

Some psychologists have compared this acceptance of suggestions and statements made with an air of authority to the bolting of food instead of masticating it as usual. Or, again, it has been compared to the taking of medicine in a capsule, the taste being hidden by the covering. No matter how it may be looked at, the fact remains that a suggestion given with the air and in the manner of one having authority has a much greater effect than the same suggestion given with an air of "everydayness," or doubt. The principle of Burr's axiom that "Truth is that which is boldly asserted, etc.," depends upon this strange fact of human psychology. The "Thus saith the Lord" manner, air, and tone of voice, has carried home many a suggestion and statement which has had but little strength in itself. The powerful suggestor is he whose attitude, manner, demeanor, tone of voice, and general expression of countenance strongly proclaims that **"There is no doubt here!"**

Hollander well says regarding this principle of suggestion: "Some people will obey any authoritative tone and manner. They are most effective on those who have never used their own wits and resources in life, but who have depended upon others for orders and instructions. The degree of suggestibility along these lines decreases as we ascend among people who have had to 'do things' for themselves, and who have not depended upon others so much."

The practitioner of Mental Suggestion will do well to preserve a gravity of demeanor and manner, and to employ positive tones of authority in giving his suggestions. His tones must carry with them the impression that he believes thoroughly in the truth of what he is saying; and that there exists not even a shadow of doubt of the desirable result to arise therefrom. He will do well to carefully study the professional air of a successful physician when diagnosing a case, and prescribing for the patient. There must always be the air of certainty, lack of doubt or indecision, and the tone of conviction. The patient is very receptive to such suggestive influences, and likewise to those of an opposite or negative character.

Association. The principle of Association is also a very important one in Mental Suggestion, as well as in every other form of mental impression or mental process. The Law of Association makes it much easier for persons to think of things in connection with other things, than to think of things by themselves. In fact, a little self-analysis will show one that he is in the habit of judging things largely by reason of their association with certain other things. And, likewise, if these certain other things be present in connection with a third thing, then that third thing is identified with the first thing even though there be but little real sameness between them.

Hollander says of this principle: "A suggestion is more likely to be successful if the idea is introduced by a person who is trusted, loved, or feared, or under circumstances that inspire these sentiments; or in a tone of voice or with a manner that one has always associated with ideas that are to be acted on or believed. One or the other of these qualities, or more often a combination of them, is an invariable characteristic of the person who is suggestive."

Therefore, the practitioner of Mental Suggestion should take care to assume the general appearance, manner, and surroundings which are associated in the mind of the patient with a successful physician. The patient associates healing of disease with certain mannerisms of the successful physician; and if the practitioner gives him the same impression he will feel more certain of the result, and of the virtue of the methods to be used. To understand this, we have but to contrast the manner of a dancing master with that of a successful surgeon; and then contrast the impression made upon the patient by each one of these two in turn; which one would have the greater associative value to the patient by the laws of suggestion? Which one would the patient have the most confidence in, and therefore gain the best results from? The student and practitioner of Mental Suggestion will do well to carefully note this point, and to employ it to his advantage in his suggestive work.

Earnestness. Earnestness has a great suggestive value. The public speaker, preacher, or lawyer who manifests earnestness and belief in what he is saying, has a decided advantage over those who fail to manifest the same suggestive principle. Earnestness and belief are more or less contagious; we are affected by these notes in the voices of those to whom we listen. The patient coming for suggestive treatment is quite sensitive to these vibrations, and is strongly responsive to the same. A few words uttered in an earnest, confident manner will accomplish far more than a long speech delivered in a manner which does not carry with it earnestness and the tone of confidence and belief.

Hollander says of this: "The quality of voice counts for more than we suspect in the relations of daily life. The speaker's power to move us depends upon his being able to create in us the feeling by which he is or pretends to be moved, and thus cause similar vibrations in our own nervous system. In this respect we are like so many musical glasses. We ring when we are in unison with the exciting object, but not otherwise. Only words that come from the heart can reach the heart. For this reason a speaker who speaks out of the fulness of his heart will be more suggestive, will create more nerve vibrations amongst his hearers than any other man who has the same amount of feeling, but cannot convey what he feels in the same manner. The more one thinks of it, the more plainly it appears that in all regions of thought the pivot on which everything turns is that of personality. What we mean by it, what importance we attach to it, colors our every idea on every subject. The personal is the one thing that interests.''

The student or practitioner of Mental Suggestion should never lose sight of the fact that earnestness in giving Suggestion makes up for many deficiencies therein; and when added to other strong qualities it becomes almost irresistible. Cultivate the air, tones, and vibrations of earnestness, and half your battle has been won. The earnest suggestor will ''get over'' even a poorly worded suggestion, whereas a suggestor lacking earnestness will be unable to impart power and dynamic force to even the most carefully expressed suggestion. Here, as in many other things in life, earnestness will often carry one through when all else fails him. It is the one quality which may be said to be **absolutely** essential in all Mental Suggestion in the treatment of physical ills. Earnestness covers up and cures a multitude of deficiencies and shortcomings in suggestion as in many other phases of mental activity. Cultivate earnestness!

Repetition. The principle of Repetition is an important one in Mental Suggestion. Indeed, it is an axiom of Mental Suggestion that **"Suggestion gains force by repetition."** It is a psychological analogy to the well-known physical examples of the repeated taps of the hammer driving the nail into the hardest wood; or of the constant dripping of the water-drops wearing away the hardest stone. Each repetition of a positive suggestion will tend to make a deeper impression upon the subconscious mind. The same suggestion repeated in different words, and with different illustrations, will serve to greatly strengthen the original induced idea.

We have examples and illustrations of this in our everyday lives. We often refuse to accept certain ideas when first presented to us, but after a while the constant repetition of them overcomes our resistance, and we end by accepting the once neglected idea; in fact, after a time we actually come to think that we have **always** believed it, if indeed we have not originated it ourselves. The constant repetition of "they say" has ruined many a good character; or, on the other hand, has built up many a fictitious reputation. Advertisers thoroughly understand this principle of psychology, and make good use of it. The constantly repeated suggestion of "Use Celluloid Soap—it's 101% Pure!" has brought us around to it eventually. Or the repeated suggestion that "You will eventually use this kind; why not now?" has done the work for many of us.

Hollander well says: "There is weakened resistance through repetition of the attack, the force of habit. We have heard certain things affirmed over and over again, until we have come to accept them as veritable facts, notwithstanding that we possess not the slightest personal knowledge of, or any logical proof regarding them. Thus public opinion is moulded."

A politician of national reputation once said: "Proof! We don't need proof! Tell the public a thing solemnly, and authoritatively, and **repeat it sufficiently often,** and you will never need to prove **anything!**"

The practitioner of Mental Suggestion should realize the value of repetition in administering therapeutic suggestion; and should carefully study out plans of stating the same thing over and over again in many ways, forms, and style of expression. Let him learn to drive the suggestive nail home by many taps—to wear away the adverse mental auto-suggestions of beliefs, by the repeated dripping of the drops of positive ideas and suggestions.

LESSON XIII

THERAPEUTIC SUGGESTION

It is a common occurrence for students to ask me for a "formula" for Mental Suggestion adapted to the requirements of Mental Healing. They seem to imagine that there is some particular grouping of words, which, when suggested into the mind of the patient, will act with a magic effect and remove all diseased conditions. In this opinion they share the blind fanaticism of some of the religious healing cults, the leaders of which give them certain "statements of truth" which, when repeated, will drive away diseased conditions and bring about normal conditions of health.

But this idea is erroneous, and clearly shows that those making such a request have not fully grasped the fundamental principle underlying the therapeutic application of Mental Suggestion. One of the first things that the student of Therapeutic Suggestion must learn is that **he must reach the mind of the patient along the accustomed channels of thought communication.** He must not insist upon creating and establishing new channels through which his suggestions may flow into the mind of the patient. To follow this last mentioned course is but to expend unnecessary time and energy. The sane and sensible plan is to first ascertain just what channels are open to him for use in this connection, and then to use them as the means of getting his positive suggestions into the mind of the patient.

This, I know, will be vigorously disputed by those who have been taught to believe in the absolute truth of some particular metaphysical or theological theory of cure; such persons will insist that the first thing necessary is to instill the Truth into the mind of the patient, and then base the subsequent treatment upon this foundation of Truth. This is all very well for those who see "Truth" crystallized into the particular teachings and doctrines of their own particular "school," cult, or "science"; but the matter takes on a different significance and meaning to those of us whose vision is sufficiently broad to grasp the fact that all of these schools, cults, and "sciences," through their respective practitioners, are making cures in about the same percentage of results—this notwithstanding that each of them has its own particular theory or doctrine which it asserts as "Truth," and as the basis of cure. Those who have grasped this fact find it logical to assume that all of these theories, doctrines, and principles **are but forms of applying some general principle of healing** which is higher than any of the particular conceptions, yet common to all of them.

The scientific student of Mental Therapeutics soon discovers that all of the formulas, methods, and wording of the various treatments of these schools, cults, and "sciences," are but the capsules in which are contained the real healing agency. He sees undoubted proof of this idea in the fact above stated, i. e., that cures are made under all these theories and methods in about the same percentage. This point once grasped, the practitioner proceeds to adapt his methods and suggestions to the particular requirements of each particular patient. He first discovers the mental and emotional characteristics of the patient, and then proceeds to use these characteristics as channels through which his suggestive treatment may flow to the mind of the patient. He becomes "all things to all men," in the best meaning of this term. He takes men as he finds them, and turns to the best account all of the personal peculiarities, characteristics, and idiosyncrasies of each of them. He takes the material before him, just as it presents itself to him, and then proceeds to work it over into what he desires it to be. He effectively applies the well-known principle of "the law of the line of least resistance."

Some may consider this an unworthy ideal and practice, but the scientific mind does not so regard it. Science has no particular theological or metaphysical conception of Absolute Truth to which it seeks to convert all comers for help, healing, and health. It has no Procrustean bed into which it must make all patients fit—stretching out the short ones and chopping off the legs of the long ones, so as to make all conform and fit into the fixed dimensions of the bed of Truth. Its only ideal of Truth is **Perfect Health;** and it endeavors to develop a practical and actual manifestation of that Truth in the minds and bodies of the patients applying to it for help and cure, instead of attempting to convert them to some particular metaphysical or theological theory.

But, here, a word of caution to students and practitioners of Mental Healing: Do not attempt to preach this doctrine of All-Truth to your patients—particularly when they first present themselves to you. First get them cured and well, and then you may give them such practical instructions regarding the Law of Cure as may seem fit for them. Do not become a zealous dispeller of illusions regarding the theory and principles underlying Suggestive Therapeutics, for this is as great a folly as that committed by those who wish to convert their patients to their own particular metaphysical or theological theories. Your business is to make cures, not to make converts—to teach Health, not doctrines or theories. Moreover, it is a fact of human nature that most persons insist upon having their Truth well dressed upon in fanciful garments, or disguised with fanciful trimmings and masks. The pure undiluted Truth has for them the alarming clearness of distilled water—they miss the familiar taste, and complain that it does not agree with them. Wise is the practitioner who figuratively asks the patient: "What flavor?" and then proceeds to give him his mental medicine disguised with the preferred flavoring and coloring.

Is this hypocrisy? Not at all; it is common sense based on experience with the race, and designed to produce the best results. Here the old aphorism, "the end justifies the means," has a striking application, in the best sense of its meaning and content. This plan is not the furthering of error, but rather the transmutation of error into actual Truth—the Truth of Perfect Health. It is the Pragmatic Method, as opposed to the Theoretical and Dogmatic Method. Its test is, "Does it work out in good results?" Not, "Is it the Absolute Truth?" And, at the last, may we not ask with Pilate the time-old question, "What is Truth?" Until Absolute Truth is discovered, let us proceed along the lines of a Working Truth—a Truth that works out in good results!

The practitioner of Mental Therapeutics will find that the patients who come to him for treatment may be grouped into the following general classes, viz.: (1) Those who incline to the belief that Divine Power is the underlying principle of the cure; (2) those who have dabbled somewhat in metaphysics, and who favor some metaphysical explanation of the cure; (3) those who are more or less familiar with the psychological principles really underlying the cure; and (4) those who are not much concerned with the underlying principle, but who rather seek the cure just as they would seek electrical treatment, massage, or even drug treatment.

The practitioner will do well to modify his treatment to fit the requirements of these different classes, which requirements he may easily ascertain by a skilful questioning of the patient at the first interview. A few leading questions will usually bring out the beliefs and opinions, the preferences and the prejudices of the patient. By following this rule the practitioner will not only make use of the deepest and widest channel of suggestion, but will also avoid antagonizing the patient by running contrary to his favorite theory and beliefs and thus setting up an unnecessary and undesirable friction or resistance. By this I do not mean that the practitioner should wilfully deceive the patient, or that he should play the hypocrite—this is not necessary or advisable, not to speak of the moral objection. Knowing the real principle employed, he may by a careful use of words in giving his suggestion practically surround his active principle with a pleasant capsule, and thus accomplish the best possible results for the patient.

The "Religious" Type

The first class, the "religious" type of patients, may be reminded that Divine Power is back of all rational treatments; and that the treatment to be given is but one of the many means which the Divine Power has placed at the disposal of suffering humanity. The terms "Divine Love," "Power of the Spirit," and other phrases familiar to this class of patients will create the very best kind of mental atmosphere for them, and will render them receptive to the healing suggestions. Religious emotion is a very powerful adjunct to suggestive treatment, as is proved by the success of those basing their healing upon the appeal to the religious feeling, faith, and belief. The statement above recommended is based upon Truth, as all but an avowed skeptic or unbeliever will admit; so that the practitioner is not deceiving the patient, nor is he playing the hypocrite, in wording his suggestions along these lines.

The "Metaphysical" Type

The second class, the metaphysical patients, will respond more readily to suggestions in which the idea that the diseased condition results from "erroneous thought," or from a lack of perception of the fact that "All is Mind." The main idea to be brought out in such cases is that the physical condition is merely the reflection of the ideas and beliefs held in the mind; and that, therefore, the restoration of the true and real mental state will result in the manifestation of a perfect physical condition. This, of course, is essentially true, although there is also a physical basis for the disease and the cure, as we have seen. Patients of this class are not interested in descriptions of the cells and organs of the body, for they prefer to regard these as more or less unreal, while Mind is the sole reality. These people seem to have a great dislike for anything suggesting physiological facts, and prefer to dwell in the thought of Mind. Accordingly, they must be reached in that way in order to be benefited.

THERAPEUTIC SUGGESTION

The "Psychological" Type

The third class, the psychological patients, are open to scientific explanations of the cause and cure of disease, such as we have considered and studied in the preceding lessons. They will grasp the explanation of the cell-minds, and the organ-minds, and will absorb, assimilate, and respond to suggestions given along those lines; while they will be repelled by the introduction of "religious talk," or "away-up-in-the-air metaphysics." Let them know just what you are seeking to accomplish, and then proceed accordingly.

The "New Thing" Type

The fourth class, the "new thing" seekers, require more or less mystery and illusion in the treatment. They like to believe that the healer has some wonderful power of mind, or otherwise, which he is going to use for their benefit. Any plausible explanation will suffice in their case, providing it is given in an authoritative manner, and in the tones of confident assurance of success. They seek the "strange, wonderful power" of the healer; and the healer who carries out this idea is the one who will obtain the best results in such cases. These people like the words "psychic power," "vital force," "magnetic power," etc., and are impressed by strange terms and methods of administering the treatment. A scientific explanation will go over their heads, and they will lose interest and accordingly will not get the best results. These people must be accepted as they are, not as they should be; the practitioner must take the raw material as he finds it, and then work it over into better things. First, last, and always, his business is to **make cures,** rather than to teach and preach to these people. This advice is based upon sound scientific psychology, and "the end justifies the means" in such cases—the "end" being the cure of the patient, and the removal of his mental and physical disorders.

LESSON XIV

WHAT TO SUGGEST TO PATIENTS

The first thing that the practitioner should suggest to the patient is, of course, the fact that he is going to get better, and then still better, and eventually get well. He should be told that the healing power is now under way, and that the process will gain force as it proceeds, each treatment adding a little further power to that which has gone before.

In a dozen different ways and forms the patient should have induced in his mind the idea and mental picture of himself as restored to perfect health. An important axiom of therapeutic suggestion is that **the suggestion should paint the picture of the desired result.** Bright pictures should be painted of the happiness, joy and general well-being which will be his when he finally acquires the desired result. And, in the same way, he should be led to look forward to each step of the way. His mind should be directed to the improvement which is sure to come as the result of the treatments. This rouses the "expectant attention," and, according to the well established psychological law of healing, will tend to manifest in an actual physical condition.

It will be found especially helpful to paint the picture of a perfectly healthy person, stress being laid upon each of the leading characteristics of such a person, so that the patient may gradually and unconsciously come to hold in his mind the picture of himself as being just this kind of person. It is a wonderful fact of psychological healing that the physical body of the patient tends to gradually grow to be just like the ideal of himself as held in his mind. In fact, the patient has probably actually pulled himself down physically by holding thoughts and mental pictures of himself as diseased, weakened, and looking wretchedly. Sick persons are fond of looking in their mirrors and then brooding over the fact that they have "fallen off," or in the idea of how wretchedly they look, physically. The more that they do this the worse do they grow; and the worse they grow the worse they look in the glass; and the worse they look in the glass, the worse mental image are they creating; and the worse mental image that they create, the worse do they get—there is a "vicious circle" of mental and physical, physical and mental, cause and effect manifested here. By creating in the mind of the patient a new and better mental image and idea of himself, the practitioner really starts into operation a "constructive circle" which works with as powerful an effect as the opposite kind just mentioned.

But this is only the beginning of the suggestive treatment, though it must be continued through all the treatments, and blended with the more specific and special suggestions which we shall presently consider. It is not enough that the patient be given **general suggestions** of health (although these alone are wonderfully efficacious, and often work marvelous cures); the practitioner must also get down to the details of the special case before him—he must go "right to the spot" of the trouble, and direct his treatments right to the point where the trouble exists.

Here is where the scientific practitioner has a great advantage over the ordinary mental healer, metaphysical healer, or religo-metaphysical healer. These healers are like a man firing a shot-gun at a mark—he may hit it with some of the scattering shot, but he does not get the powerful effect secured by the man using a rifle with a big bullet backed by a strong explosive charge. The scientific practitioner is the man with the powerful rifle—when he hits the mark the effect is clearly perceptible; and by preparation and practice he learns to hit the mark nearly every time. The general treatment (and this he should also use, as we have said) is like a shell filled with scattering shot; when to this is added the rifle ball of a special scientific treatment, it is hard to conceive of a successful result not being obtained.

It is for this reason that in later lessons of this course we shall indicate the principal classes of physical disorders and diseases, giving the physiological and psychological characteristics of each. By an acquaintance with these principal classes of diseases, the student of Mental Therapy is enabled to diagnose the root of the trouble, and then to direct his suggestion directly to the mind in the affected parts, without "scatteration" of force, or waste of energy. This does not mean that he should, like drug doctors, keep his thought fixed on the diseased condition (for this is contrary to all the principle of mental healing); but on the other hand he should direct his attention to the affected part so that he may begin building up in his own mind, and that of the patient, a picture and ideal of the normal and healthy condition of the organ and part, and to play upon that organ or part all of the mental power at his command, to the end that normal and natural conditions and functioning may be restored and firmly established, the result being Health and Cure.

In studying the later lessons just referred to, the student will discover that imperfect functioning of the main organs of nutrition, and those of elimination, is the real cause of a multitude of physical ills, many of which are seated at points in the body far removed from the seat of the real cause and trouble. The scientific practitioner by a knowledge of this fact is enabled to remove the real root of the trouble, whereupon the entire trouble withers and passes away. Such a practitioner does not waste time and energy in treating symptoms, but rather seeks to destroy the root of the evil conditions. The average practitioner knows nothing at all about these things, and is unable to produce the desired result in a short time; in reality, considering these facts, it is a wonderful proof of the efficacy of Mental Therapeutic principles that such practitioners and healers make the cures they do—

they make them in spite of their ignorance; what wonderful results are possible of accomplishment by the trained, scientific practitioner!

So true is the above statement regarding the effect of improper functioning on the part of the main organs of nutrition, and those of elimination, that I strongly advise all practitioners of mental healing to always give the treatment indicated for troubles of this kind, even when there does not seem to be any evidence of such trouble. It will be found that such treatment will speedily improve the general condition of the patient, and will build up his general physical health to such an extent that the other troubles may be easily removed. The building-up of the main organs of nutrition, and those of elimination, gives a tone to the whole system; it increases the natural resistive powers of the Corporeal Mind, and thus makes it much easier to throw off the other abnormal conditions. More than this, by relieving Nature of her work in combating the imperfect conditions existing in the main organs of nutrition, and those of elimination, we give Nature a chance to throw more of her recuperative power into the other affected parts. The importance of this is seen when we remember that when we say "Nature" in this connection we are really speaking of the Corporeal Mind which has all the physical functions under its direct control and management.

In giving therapeutic suggestions, the practitioner will always find it of benefit to hold in his mind the idea that **he is talking directly to the**

Corporeal Mind of the patient. He need not tell the patient this, for it would involve him in a long and technical explanation and discussion. Let the patient think that the practitioner means his ordinary everyday self when he says "You" in giving the suggestions; but let the practitioner hold in his own mind the idea and thought that when he says "You" (in the suggestive treatment) he is really addressing the Corporeal Mind. And, also let him picture that Corporeal Mind as having a mentality something like that of **an intelligent, bright, and dutiful young child,** with whom he is quite friendly. Strange as it may appear to those who know nothing about the inner explanation of the matter, it is a fact that the Corporeal Mind will "make up" to the practitioner who will thus open up friendly communication with it. At first a little shy, like the young child, it will become friendly and desirous of helping the practitioner in his work of healing. This is a very strange fact of therapeutic psychology; but it is one that every practitioner may ascertain for himself—and fortunate, indeed, is that practitioner who is able to grasp the truth of this principle and who will apply it in actual practice.

More than this, it is a fact that each and every organ of the body has its own distinct personality (if this term may be used in this connection). And, also, the suggestionist may actually address his suggestions to the different organs, by concentrating his attention upon them and using the word "You" in that sense when addressing his suggestions to the patient. Here, again, it is not well to say anything about this to the patient, for the reasons previously stated. The healer who holds in mind this idea that he is directly addressing the particular organ or part of the body, is often able to reach into the very soul of that organ (if we are allowed to use this term in this connection), and thus persuade it to put forth its best energies in the work of cure.

Careful students and practitioners of Mental Therapeutics have discovered that not only is there a personality in each organ-mind, but that also this personality varies according to the character of the work performed by the organ in question. For instance, it has been discovered that the Liver is more or less stupid, as compared with the other organs; it is heavy and dense mentally, and needs to be spoken to sharply, and sometimes even harshly, in order to get it to work properly; it is more like a pig than is any other organ of the body—and it must be treated accordingly.

The personality of the Heart, on the contrary, is like that of a high-spirited, intelligent horse; and the methods used in the case of the Liver would be entirely out of place in treating the Heart. The personality of the Stomach is something like that of a good-natured, faithful dog; it has confidence in those it likes, and when patiently taught to do a thing it will be glad to obey orders to the best of its ability. These distinctions, and others. will be brought out in the latter lessons—I am merely directing them to your attention in this place, in order that you may file them away in your memory in connection with the subject now being considered.

A leading American writer on the subject has said: "The way to reach the mind in the cells, cell-groups, ganglia, organs, nerves, parts, etc., of the body is to **address yourself directly to it, just as you would to a person.** You must think of the mind in the affected part as a 'person' who is misbehaving. You must remonstrate with it, argue with it, coax, order or drive the 'person' residing in the organ, just as you would with different individuals. Sometimes coaxing is much better than driving, but sometimes forceful methods are necessary. * * * Tell the cell-mind just what you expect of it—just what you intend it shall do—just what it is right for it to do—**and it will obey!**" I trust that every practitioner will make this knowledge his own, and apply it in his actual healing work, using many forms of disguising it if necessary; for it is one of the greatest of the recent discoveries of Mental Therapeutics, and produces wonderful effects when properly and intelligently applied.

LESSON XV

THERAPEUTIC AUTO-SUGGESTION

As these lessons are designed to teach self-healing by the principles of Mental Therapeutics as well as the healing of others by the employment of the same principle, I have thought it advisable to insert at this particular place in the course a lesson devoted to Auto-Suggestion as applied to self-healing. I shall follow the same course when we come to the proper point in the study of the succeeding phases of Mental Healing.

By Auto-Suggestion in general is meant the employment of Mental Suggestion directed to one's own subconscious mind; or, in the present case, the employment of Mental Suggestion directed to one's own Corporeal Mind. In this form of Mental Suggestion, the person enacts the dual role of suggestor and suggestee—the one making the suggestions, and the one receiving the suggestions, both at the same time. So true is this in fact that in Therapeutic Auto-Suggestion each and every one of the principles of Mental Suggestion, as applied to other persons, which we have considered in the preceding lessons, are applicable to the requirements of the person himself when he is treating himself by Auto-Suggestion. To all intents and purposes the person being treated (who is also the person giving the treatment, of course) is to be considered as a distinct entity, or different person.

This may seem somewhat confusing to the student, at least at first; but when the psychology of the process is analyzed it will be seen as being as strictly natural and scientific as is any other form of Mental Suggestion. The secret of the whole process is found in the fact that in Auto-Suggestion **the conscious "I" suggests to the subconscious "Me."** When you have grasped this principle you have gained the secret of all true Therapeutic Auto-Suggestion. And, until you have fully grasped this fact, you will not be able to apply the principles of Therapeutic Auto-Suggestion effectively.

In order to get the best effects of Therapeutic Auto-Suggestion, you should make a clear mental distinction between the conscious self which is giving the suggestions and the subconscious self which is receiving them. You should actually visualize the "I" suggesting and giving orders to the "Me." You should visualize the subconscious "Me" as a distinct entity, subordinate to the "I," and should give your suggestions in that spirit. So true is this that the best authorities now advise that in giving Therapeutic Auto-Suggestion the person should actually address the subconscious "Me" by name, instead of saying "I" in giving the Auto-Suggestion.

This idea of addressing the subconscious mind as a separate entity, and using a name in doing so, was first suggested by William Walker

THERAPEUTIC AUTO-SUGGESTION

Atkinson, an American writer on the subject, about ten years ago; the idea being developed in greater detail in his later writings. It has been taken up and adopted by many subsequent writers on the subject, and is now employed by many American and European teachers of various forms of Therapeutic Auto-Suggestion under some name or guise. In one of his works this authority says of this principle previously announced by himself:

"I have always contended that there is a much better way of making the affirmation or auto-suggestion, than the familiar 'I am this, or that.' I have found that the nearer one comes to the perfect playing-out of the dual role of suggestor and suggestee, the better will be the result, and the clearer the impression made upon the subconscious mind. Accordingly, one should endeavor to 'talk to himself' just as if he were speaking to some other person. He should give his suggestions to himself precisely as if he were suggesting to another person. Whatever may be the explanation of this psychological process, the fact remains that by following this course the person will be able to register a much clearer, deeper, and more lasting impression than by using the 'I am this or that' form of affirmation or auto-suggestion. In fact, I think that the idea of 'affirmation' may as well be discarded, first and last, in the practical work of Auto-Suggestion, and that the 'I' of the person should actually suggest to the subconscious

'Me' of himself. Let it be 'suggestion,' instead of 'affirmation.'

"In making these suggestions to yourself, you should always address yourself as if you were speaking to a third person. Instead of saying 'I am courageous and fearless,' you should suggest to yourself as follows: 'John Smith (here use your own name, of course), you are courageous and fearless; you fear nothing; every day you are gaining in courage and fearlessness, and are getting stronger, stronger, stronger, every day you live, etc.' Do you get the idea? Try both methods now—interrupting your reading for the purpose. Make as strong an 'I' affirmation as you can, and then try the effect of the strongest suggestion of the 'John Smith, you are, etc.,' kind, addressed to your subconscious 'Me.' Imagine that you are addressing and suggesting to another person whom you are very desirous of building up and strengthening. You will find a new field of Auto-Suggestion opening up before you. A little knack is required, but a few trials will show you the value of this improved method. Talk to 'John Smith' as if he were an entirely different individual. Tell him what you wish him to do and become, and how you expect him to act. You will be surprised to see how obedient this subconscious mentality will become. You will find that by this plan you will be able to fairly pour the positive suggestions into the receptive subconscious mind—and that the 'John Smith' part of you will accept the impressions just as if there were actually two persons taking part in the process, instead of merely one. This is not mere childish play or make-believe—it is a process based upon the soundest psychological principles."

In a public address of the authority just quoted, in which this subject was introduced, the speaker said: "Continued experience has convinced me that I was on the right track when 1 enunciated this principle of Auto-Suggestion, and I am not surprised at the popularity it has since attained. I have very little to add to the principle and method as originally stated. I may add, however, that from the reports of many persons who have experimented with this method in their own cases I have come to the conviction that the best effects are secured when the auto-suggestor addresses himself by some familiar nickname, or abbreviation of his name, which has been used in his childhood days. It would seem that by the use of the name familiar to the mind in the days of its early development, one is able to penetrate to deeper levels of subconsciousness than even by the use of the formal name used in later years. In such cases then, instead of 'John Smith,' let us say, 'Here, you, **Jack** Smith,' or 'Here you, **Reddy** Smith'—or, in short, **whatever name seems to sink in the deepest.**"

The principle of addressing the organ-minds in suggestion has also been extended to Auto-Suggestion by the same authority, and those who . have adopted his methods and principles of treatment. It will be found effective to address the mind in the troubled organ just as if it were really an entity, and to direct the suggestions directly to it. It may be found well to gently tap the body directly over the location of the organ in question, using the tips of the fingers for the purpose—something like giving a gentle tap at the door before venturing to enter the room. This seems to have a peculiar psychological effect in the direction of arousing and attracting the attention of the organ-mind; and thereafter the "talk" to the organ-mind will have a much greater effect.

For instance, if you are troubled with an inactive Liver, you should tap a little over the place where the Liver is located, a little more in the case of the Liver than in the case of some other organs—for the Liver is slow, stubborn, and hard to arouse; remember, we have compared it to a pig, and it must be treated like a pig-mind. Tap, tap, tap, until the sleepy, lazy Liver is aroused and cocks its ears in your direction. Then say to it: "Here, Liver, you wake up and listen to me; wake up and listen, I tell you; wake up right now and listen to me! You haven't been doing your work properly; you have been too sluggish and lazy about it; you have got to do better, I tell you, got to do better; do you hear me? I am feeding you well, and keeping you comfortable, and not giving you any more work to do than you should do; and I expect you to perform your natural work properly. Get busy now, and do your work properly; I insist upon you doing your work properly, and I intend keeping after you until you do. Come now, get busy, and do your work, for I intend prodding you up until you do it. You ought to be ashamed of yourself for acting that way! But you're going to do better from now on; better from now on, I tell you!" This may seem foolish; but just try it on a sluggish Liver and see how well it works. Of course, you should treat your Liver right, and not impose unnatural tasks upon it by eating improperly; treat it right, and insist that it treats you right. You can often actually feel the Liver-mind "getting busy" after a treatment of this kind.

The Stomach may be addressed in a similar way; but you must remember that the Stomach is not a piggish animal like the Liver. On the contrary, as I have said elsewhere, it is more like a good-natured old-fashioned Newfoundland dog, which is desirous of pleasing its master, and who will respond readily to kindness and confidence. Treat the Stomach right, and let it know that you have confidence in it and faith that it will perform its work of digesting your food properly—and then notice the improvement in this respect. The trouble with many persons is that they have so abused their stomachs that it has grown discouraged—its spirit is broken, like that of an abused dog. It feels that "nobody loves me," and that its owner is always ready to beat and abuse it. Change your mental attitude toward your Stomach, and let it know that you have done so, and then notice how quickly it responds, and how glad it is to do what you want, so long as you do not impose unnatural tasks upon it.

In the same way the Bowels will respond to coaxing mixed with firmness. You have probably discouraged them by refusing to heed their calls, and they have "laid down on the job." Reform yourself, and you will reform them; but you will have to let them know the new condition of affairs before they will take up new habits. Tell them that you expect them to operate at a certain time of the day, and that you will faithfully attend to your part of the bargain; keep this up until the new habit is firmly established.

As we proceed, you will learn about the treatment of other ills by Mental Therapeutics; and you may apply to your own case, by Auto-Suggestion and otherwise, all the methods described as efficacious when applied to other persons by means of Suggestion and other ways. The principle is one—the only difference is that of the means of application. **Any principle that may be applied to the treatment of a patient may also be applied by you in your own case, by means of Auto-Suggestion,** along the lines indicated in this lesson. Do not forget this fact!

LESSON XVI

THOUGHT INDUCTION

The second and third general classes of the methods of applying Mental Healing are (a) Personal Thought Induction, and (b) Distant Thought Induction, respectively. These two methods are based on the same general principle, i. e., that of the induction of the healing thoughts of the practitioner into the subconscious mind of the patient; but there are certain distinctions between the two methods which justify their classification as separate methods and processes of application.

In the present lesson we shall consider the first of these two methods of Thought Induction, namely, that of Personal Thought Induction. Here we have to do with cases of Thought Induction in which the practitioner is in the actual physical presence of the patient, just as when Mental Suggestion is given. In fact, Personal Thought Induction may be spoken of here as practically **Mental Suggestion without the use of words written, printed, or spoken**. Here the thoughts, or ideas, of the practitioner are radiated from his mind, and then, coming in contact with the mind of the patient, they are transformed into corresponding ideas or mental pictures in that mind.

The thoughts, ideas, or mental pictures held in the mind of the practitioner, and then radiated or transmitted to the mind of the patient, should be practically the same as those expressed in words by the suggestionist in Mental Suggestion. That is to say, the practitioner should create in his own mind the thought, idea, or mental picture of the same normal, healthy conditions which he seeks to suggest into the mind of the patient. He should see not only the patient as in good normal health, but also as having perfect healthy organs functioning naturally and efficiently. In the degree that he is able to form such clear, strong, positive thoughts, ideas, or mental pictures, so will be the degree of the success of his mental treatments along these lines.

And, now, a few words regarding the scientific explanation of this radiation of thought, ideas, and mental pictures from the mind of one person to that of another. It is, of course, impossible to give the ultimate explanation of this wonderful phenomenon—or any other for that matter. Until we are able to state the "just what" of anything—the absolute and ultimate nature of that thing—we must content ourselves with the statement of "just how" the thing works and acts. And, so, here I shall not attempt to explain just what Mind or Thought really is, in its absolute and ultimate nature (who, indeed, is able to do this?), but shall, instead, try to explain just how Mind or Thought works and manifests in this process of Thought Induction.

But, notwithstanding the impossibility of explaining the "thing-in-itselfness" behind the process and manifestation, we are clearly within our powers and rights when we venture to compare this class of phenomena with certain other phenomena with which we are more familiar. The very word "induction" gives us the key to this.

The definition of the term "Induction," as used in Physics, is as follows: **"The property or process by which one body having electrical or magnetic polarity produces it in another body without direct contact."** A text-book on the subject informs us that "Electric induction is the action which electrified bodies exert **at a distance** on bodies in a natural state; Magnetic Induction is the action which magnetized bodies exert **at a distance** on bodies in a natural state." The same authority informs us that the technical meaning of the term "Induce" is: "To cause by proximity **without contact or transmission;** for example, the production of a particular electric or magnetic condition in a body, by placing another body in an opposite electric state, in proximity to it **but without actual contact."** An "Induced Current" is: "An electrical current developed in a conductor **in proximity to, but not in contact with,** other conductors traversed by intermittent or fluctuating currents; also, electric currents developed in conductors moving **in the field** of a magnet, or in conductors **within the field** of a moving magnet." "Inductive Power is the name given by Faraday to the property which bodies possess of transmitting the electric influence."

So, you see, that in the case of electricity and

magnetism we have a striking analogy to the process by which positive Thought induces in another mind similar Thought, providing that the second mind comes within the "field of induction," or "field of influence" of the first mind. You will note that in the case of pure induction, in electricity or magnetism, there is no passage of an actual current such as travels along the electric wire or other conductors; but rather a strange and unaccountable "stirring up" of power in the second object which comes within the field of induction of the first one. In fact, in such induction the electrical current is set up in a second conductor which is in proximity to, but not in contact with, a first conductor **—the power is induced in conductors without the necessity of a connecting conductor.**

But, it may be urged, there is no proof that Thought radiates power in this way. Isn't there? Outside of the enormous mass of proof gathered by the various scientific societies investigating this class of phenomena, and that of private individuals working along the same line, there is the testimony of recent advanced science that **all substances are radio-active,** and the proofs of the scientific laboratories that the brain is not only radio-active, but that its activities register on delicate photographic plates specially prepared. There is nothing more wonderful in thought-radiation than there is in the radiation of electricity, magnetism, light or heat—one is as wonderful as the other, though familiarity has made certain forms of radiation seem more commonplace than the others.

Above the scale of light vibrations visible to the human eye there are vast fields of light vibrations which science recognizes by the report of delicate scientific instruments. In the field of the ultra-violet light rays lie many strange forms of chemical rays, and rays which cannot be classified, though they are registered by delicate instruments. An American writer says of these: "In this ultra-violet region lie the 'X-rays,' and the other recently discovered high-degree rays; also the actinic rays, which, while invisible to the eye, register on the photographic place, sunburn one's face, blister one's nose, and even cause violent explosions in chemical substances exposed to them, as well as acting on the green leaves of plants, causing the chemical change of transforming carbonic acid and water into sugar and starches. These forms of 'dark light,' that is, light too fine to be perceived by the human eye, are but faint indications of the existence of still higher and finer vibrations— the 'finer forces of nature.' "

Professor Ochorowicz, one of the world's great scientists, comes out with a positive statement of belief in Thought Induction, and in one of his works he advances a general working theory of the action of Thought-Force in this way. He says: "Every living being is a dynamic focus. A dynamic focus tends ever to propagate the motion that is proper to it. Propagated motion becomes transformed according to the medium it traverses.   Motion tends always to propagate itself.   Therefore, when we see work of any kind—mechanical, electrical, nervic, or psychic —disappear without visible effect, then, of two things, one happens, either a transmission or a transformation.   Where does the first end, and where does the second begin?   In an identical medium there is only **transmission.**   In a different medium there is **transformation.**   You send an electrical current through a thick wire.   You have the current, but you do not perceive any other force.   But cut that thick wire and connect the ends by means of a fine wire; the fine wire will grow hot; there will be a transformation of a part of the current into heat.   Take a pretty strong current and interpose a wire still more resistant, or a very thin carbon rod, and the carbon will emit light.   A part of the current, then, is transformed into heat and light. This light acts in every direction around about, first visibly as light, then invisibly as heat and electric current.   Hold a magnet near it.   If the magnet is weak and movable, in the form of a magnetic needle, the beam of light will cause it to deviate; if it is strong and immovable, it will in turn cause the beam of light to deviate.   **And all this from a distance, without contact, without special conductors.**

"A process that is once chemical, physical and psychical, goes on in the brain.   A complex action of this kind is propagated through the gray matter, as waves are propagated in water. Regarded on its physiological side, an idea is only a vibration, a vibration that is propagated, yet which does not pass out of a medium in which it can exist as such. It is propagated as far as other vibrations allow. It is propagated more widely, if it assumes the character which subjectively we call emotive. **But it cannot go beyond without being transformed.** Nevertheless, like force in general, it cannot remain in isolation, it escapes in disguise. Thought stays at home, as the chemical action of a battery remains in the battery; it is represented by its dynamic correlate, called in the case of the battery a **current;** and in the case of the brain, I know not what. But whatever its name may be, it is **the dynamic correlate of thought.**

"A force that is transmitted meets other forces, and if it is transformed only little by little it usually limits itself to modifying another force at its own cost, though without suffering perceptibly thereby. This is the case particularly with forces that are persistent, concentrated, well seconded by their medium. **This is the case with the physiological equilibrium, nervic force, psychic force, ideas, emotions, tendencies. These modify environing forces, without themselves disappearing. They are imperceptibly transformed, and, if the next man is of a nature exceptionally well adapted to them, they gain in inductive action.**"

Professor Bain, the eminent authority upon "Mind and Body," calls our attention to the following very significant fact: "The structure of the nervous substances, and the experiments made upon the nerves and nerve-centers, establish beyond doubt certain peculiarities as belonging to the force that is exercised by the brain. This force is of a current nature; that is to say, a power generated at one part of the structure is conveyed along an intervening substance and discharged at some other part. The different forms of electricity and magnetism have made us familiar with this kind of action."

But, most of us who are studying Mental Therapeutics have satisfied ourselves with the fact of the phenomenon of Thought Induction. The above scientific statements are offered not as proof, but merely to give a practical working hypothesis to those whose minds require the same in order to reason deductively from principle to manifestation. Let us pass on from this stage of the subject to that of the "just how to" practice Thought Induction in our work of Mental Healing. A little theory is a good thing to serve as a base and a foundation, but we must not spend all of our time on foundations—rather should we proceed to erect a structure of practical results upon the firm foundation of hypothesis and scientific principles.

LESSON XVII

THE PRACTICE OF THOUGHT-INDUCTION

In giving treatments along the lines of Personal Thought Induction, the practitioner should always bear in mind this one fundamental principle of practice, viz., **Thought Induction is silent Mental Suggestion.** With this fundamental principle once firmly fixed in his mind, the practitioner will not likely go very far wrong in giving the treatments.

There is, of course, a little practice required in order that the practitioner may acquire confidence and ease, and get rid of the awkwardness which usually attends the practice of unfamiliar processes. He will do well to practice and rehearse before a mirror, or when alone by himself, in order to acquire a confident bearing and ease of manner when giving treatments of this kind.

Many practitioners who have received personal instruction from me have gained great benefit from practicing the treatment before a mirror along the general lines indicated below.

Practice Exercise: Stand before your mirror, and treat your reflected image therein just as if it were another person. Begin by treating it for any complaint which may occur to you. You run no risk whatsoever in doing this—no danger of "taking on" a complaint—for your treatments are always **constructive** and upbuilding, and never along the lines of diseased conditions. In practice, and in actual treatments, you should **always hold the mental picture of the desired condition**—not that of the diseased condition; and always make your silent suggestions along the lines of positive upbuilding, **stating the conditions you wish to produce,** and never those which you wish to remove. **Always point out the mental road you wish the Corporeal Mind to follow.**

In practicing before the mirror, you should throw yourself into the exercise in full earnestness. Do not indulge in flippant and frivolous play regarding treatments—throw earnestness into your thoughts and mental pictures. Do not merely think the **idea** of what you wish to silently suggest to the imaginary patient; but actually think the **words** in which you would express the idea if you were speaking to the patient. This formation of **words** in the mind, and the projection of them in Thought Induction is very important. There is, of course, no magic in the words themselves, but nevertheless the action of the mind in crystallizing the idea into words gives concentrated force to them, and they are projected with greatly increased power into the mind of the patient. In giving Thought Induction treatments then, remember to **think in actual words.** Form the actual words in your mind.

In these practice exercises, and in **giving** actual treatments to patients while in their presence, you should follow the same general **rules**

which are followed in giving audible Mental Suggestion. That is to say, you should throw the same degree of earnestness into the silent words that you would in the spoken words. You should encourage the same feeling of force and power within yourself—the same raising of your own vibrations so that they may become positive to those of the patient. You should remember the principle of Repetition, as mentioned in connection with Mental Suggestion; and manage to repeat the same silent mental commands or suggestions a number of times.

Remember, always, that **you are actually and really addressing the Corporeal Mind of the patient in these silent treatments,** just as truly as when you address the conscious mind of the person in an ordinary spoken course of instructions, commands or advice. The more that you are able to realize this actual process the more force and power will you manifest. The subconscious mind, in all of its phases, is very quick to sense the degree of earnestness and belief, or the degree of lightness and unbelief, in the mind of the practitioner; and it responds in the same degree. It is like a child or an intelligent animal —very keen to perceive shades of feeling or belief, truth or untruth.

In giving actual treatments by Personal Thought Induction, you should instruct the patient to sit quietly in a comfortable position— have a cozy, comfortable chair in your treating-room for this purpose. It is well to have your treating-room as quiet as possible, and as free

as possible from disturbing influences. It is well to have the light somewhat dim or shaded, for bright lights tend to distract the attention. The main idea in fitting up the room and furnishing it should be that of inducing the idea of Quiet, Poise, Calm, and Peace.

Bid the patient to sit quietly and easily; and to relax himself completely, taking the tension off every muscle, and every strain off the mind. You will be able to help him in this matter by sitting quietly some little distance from him, and placing yourself in the proper mental attitude. Sit quietly yourself, stilling your own feelings and thoughts, and you will gradually raise up your vibrations from the lower plane to that of Peace, Harmony, and Health. The patient will then sense these vibrations and will experience a feeling of Calmness and Peace; this stage is often marked by the patient giving utterance to a gentle sigh of relief, and a further relaxing of mind and body.

The desired mental condition having been produced in the patient, the practitioner should form a strong mental image or picture of the patient before him and presenting all the outward appearances of perfect health; he should see the patient as a strong, healthy, vigorous, happy man or woman. The practitioner should keep this idea or mental picture before him as much as possible during the entire treatment. He should refuse to think of or picture the patient in a condition of disease or weakness;

but should always insist upon his mind picturing the desired condition of health.

Then he should begin making the silent suggestions of the desired conditions—the conditions which he wishes to have manifested in actual physical substance and form in the body of the patient. He should address the Corporeal Mind of the patient just as he would an actual entity. He may even address it as "Mind," just as he would a person; and then tell "Mind" what he wishes it to do for the patient. He may further likewise address the organ-minds, or cell-minds of the body of the patient, just as he would do in Mental Suggestion, or in Auto-Suggestion. The principles of healing are always the same, remember, notwithstanding the differences in the forms of administering it.

In my own experiments and actual practice conducted for the purpose of developing and perfecting the methods which I teach to my students, as well as in the work that I have had my students perform under my direction, I have found the following general method or idea to work out very effectively in this class of treatments. You will note that this general method is not so much a matter of saying or doing a certain thing as it is a **case of holding a certain mental attitude.** This fact may prejudice some against it, by causing them to regard the idea as fanciful or even fantastic. But those who have pondered these things deeply, and who have grasped certain little-known underlying principles of the action of the subconscious mind,

MENTAL THERAPEUTICS

have no such illusions or misconceptions—instead, they realize that this general method has as its foundation a very basic fact of the operation of the subconscious mentality of man, particularly of that phase which is known as the Corporeal Mind.

The method, or general idea, above referred to is simply this, viz.: **The practitioner must take the mental position, and assume the mental attitude, that the physical body of the patient, in its entirety and in its parts, down even to the cells composing it, is PLASTIC SUBSTANCE which may be molded by the thought influence and power of himself (the practitioner), just as the plastic clay is molded by the hands of the potter or the sculptor.** The mental images and ideas projected from the mind of the practitioner, and the silent suggestions made by him in this form of treatment, are to be regarded as the tools of the potter or sculptor; and are to be used to shape up this part, mold this one, reduce that one, and energize and vitalize the other one. Under the silent force of the creative mind of the practitioner, the physical body of the patient must be thought of as being built-up, strengthened, and restored to normal functioning; the parts thought of as being built up and energized; the cells thought of as doing their work with renewed energy and activity; and the whole system flooded with vital force and energy, vitality and life. Under the strong stimulus of this thought, image, and ideal held in the mind of the practitioner, the body of the patient should respond to the ideals of the practitioner, and should develop in strength, vigor and general health.

This same principle, or rather all of the principles described in this lesson, may be used by the person wishing to heal himself by means of Self-Treatment. What the mind of a healer can do for a patient, the mind of the patient can do for himself, **providing he has the perseverance and persistence** to carry out the principles of cure as set forth in these lessons. The principle of Self-Healing by this method is precisely the same as that of the treatment of the patient by the practitioner.

In Self-Treatment the person should follow the methods and forms of treatment set forth in the lesson on Auto-Suggestion, and also those recited in the present lesson. That is to say, he should not only actually suggest to himself in the way described in the lesson on Auto-Suggestion, but he should also cultivate the art of visualizing or picturing himself as possessing a perfect, healthy, strong body, functioning perfectly in every organ, and perfect in every part. To this he should add the habit of refusing to think of his body as weak, diseased, or imperfect in any way. **He should acquire the habit of thinking of his body as already being that which he wishes it to be.**

To those who may object that this seems like a case of wilfully trying to deceive oneself, and to delude oneself as to real facts concerning the body, I would say that such is but a narrow view to take of the matter. Self-deception does no one any good—we do not escape evils by refusing to see them when they are present—there is no question about this. But when we come to deal with the Corporeal Mind we have another state of affairs to deal with. The Corporeal Mind has the tendency **to manifest into physical form the mental images concerning it which are habitually held in the mind of a person.** This is no idle fantasy—it is a scientific fact. Therefore, if the Corporeal Mind has followed after bad patterns, **it is necessary for us to hold before it the pattern of the conditions which we wish it to manifest,** if we wish to regain the normal natural condition. And, at the last, the normal, natural condition of the body is TRUTH, and we are fully justified in insisting that the Corporeal Mind cast off the result of its imperfect and erroneous patterns, and instead adopt the perfect pattern of that which nature intended us to be, of that which is Truth. We have a right to hold fast to the idea that the Power-that-Is wishes to manifest in the Good, the Beautiful, and the True—and that all else is a perversion of the intent of nature; and to insist that the pattern of Truth be followed as a design, not that of Error and Untruth. This may sound somewhat metaphysical, but it is based upon the report of the great minds of the race, and we may demonstrate it by actual practice.

.LESSON XVIII

DISTANT THOUGHT-INDUCTION

The third general class of the methods of practicing Mental Healing is that known as Distant Thought Induction. In this form of treatment the thought-vibrations of the practitioner are carried to great distances in space to the patient. In fact, so far as has been discovered, space is practically wiped out in this class of thought induction; it has been found that it is just as easy to treat a patient ten thousand miles away as one a hundred yards distant, by this method of treatment.

In Distant Thought Induction the principle employed is precisely the same as that employed in Personal Thought Induction, plus the manifestation of certain mental activities which serve to carry the thought-vibrations beyond the usual limits of Thought Induction. As I have said elsewhere in these lessons, Distant Thought Induction is akin to the telescope or the telephone, inasmuch as it enables a natural faculty to manifest at a distance otherwise impossible for it.

It will be seen at first glance that the possibilities of Mental Healing are enormously increased by the discovery that Thought masters and annihilates space. So true is this that the greater part of the Mental Healing of this day is performed by this method. Some healers will not receive personal patients, but give all of their treatments in this way; they claim that they can obtain far better results, by reason of the concentration possible only in this form of treatment, and the obviating of the disturbing influences of the personal presence of the patient. So important is this phase of Mental Healing that the student and practitioner should pay special attention to its theory, principles, and methods of application and manifestation. I shall go into this subject deeply and thoroughly in this and the following lessons.

There are those who while fully accepting the fact that Thought is radio-active, and that our mental vibrations surround us with a mental atmosphere, and that this mental atmosphere constitutes our field of mental induction which awakens similar vibrations in the minds of others coming within its influence, nevertheless find it difficult to accept the teachings that assert that Thought may be sent to a distance far from the sender, and there be received by the mind of another person.

I cannot understand why anyone should feel any doubt on this score, for the last mentioned phenomenon is not a whit more wonderful or mysterious than is the simplest case of mental induction when the two persons are in personal contact, or in near proximity to each other. We have the very closest kind of analogy in the case of electricity. In electricity we have the transmission of the current over the telegraph or telephone wires; in Thought we have a similar transmission over the wires of the nervous system reaching to all parts of the body. In electricity we have the induction of a current without direct transmission, as described in a preceding lesson; in Thought we have a similar induction of Thought without direct transmission, as also described in the said lesson. Finally, in electricity we have the transmission of a current, without the presence of wires, as we see in the case of the wireless telegraph process; in Thought we have Distant Thought Induction, or Telepathy at a distance. All of these phases of electricity are but forms of manifestation of one general principle; and all these phases of Thought Induction are but forms of manifestation of one general principle. The analogy is one of those very striking instances of the operation of the Law of Correspondence in the phenomenal world.

To those who may consider the above analogy as lacking in scientific validity, I would refer the following statement made in the presidential address of Sir William Crookes before the Royal Society, at Bristol, England, nearly twenty years ago—far in advance of the times, of course. Crookes said: "If telepathy takes place, we have two physical facts—the physical change in the brain of A, the suggestor, and the analogous physical change in the brain of B, the recipient of the suggestion. Between these two physical events there must exist a train of physical causes. * * * All the phenomena of the universe are presumably in some way continuous, and it is unscientific to call in the aid of mysterious agencies when with every fresh advance in knowledge it is shown that ether vibrations have powers and attributes abundantly equal to any demand—even the transmission of thought.

"It is supposed by some physiologists that the essential cells of nerves do not actually touch, but are separated by a narrow gap which widens in sleep while it narrows almost to extinction during mental activity. This condition is so singularly like that of a Branly or Lodge coherer [a device which led to the discovery of wireless telegraphy] as to suggest a further analogy. The structure of brain and nerve being similar, it is conceivable that **there may be present masses of such nerve coherers in the brain whose special function it may be to receive.** impulses from without through the connecting sequence of ether waves of appropriate order of magnitude.

"Roentgen has familiarized us with an order of vibrations of extreme minuteness compared with the smallest waves with which we have hitherto been acquainted, and of dimensions comparable with the distances between the centers of the atoms of which the material universe is built up; and there is no reason to suppose that we have here reached the limit of frequency. It is known that the action of thought is accompanied by certain molecular movements in the brain, and here we have physical vibrations capable from their extreme minuteness of acting direct on individual molecules, while their rapidity approaches that of the internal and external movements of the atoms themselves. A formidable range of phenomena must be scientifically sifted before we effectually grasp a faculty so strange, so bewildering, and for ages so inscrutable as the direct action of mind upon mind."

So, we see that there is the very best kind of scientific basis for asserting the analogy between the wireless telegraph on the one hand, and the phenomenon of Distant Thought Induction on the other. Nature is fond of establishing these correspondences on different planes of her activities, that we may understand one by studying the other. The more that we learn about wireless telegraphy the more readily may we understand distant thought transference and induction.

Sir William Crookes has given us many other reasons why distant thought transmission is possible. For instance, he has said: "If we accept the theory that the brain is composed of separate elements—nerve cells—then we must presume that each of these components, like every other bit of matter, has its movements of vibration and will under suitable conditions be affected; as, for instance, the nerve cells of the retina by vibration in the ether. If another neuron situated not far away should acquire the same movement of vibration, there seems to be no good reason why they should not affect each other through the ether."

Edward T. Bennett, the English psychologist, has said: "The conclusion seems to be irresistible that the five senses do not exhaust the means by which knowledge may enter the mind. In other words, the investigator seems to be driven to the conclusion that thought-transference or telepathy must now be included among scientifically proven facts.''

Professor Quackenbos, the American psychologist, says: ''The time has indeed come, as Maeterlinck predicted it would, when souls may know each other without the intermediary of the senses.''

Clark Bell says: ''Telepathy, as it is regarded by scientists who accept it as a fact, is some unknown sense of power in the human body, by which as a physical process communication is held between brain and brain of the human organism—some means by which the perceptions are reached in some manner analogous to the known and well-defined transmission of the electric current, or the action of gravitation, which we know exists. But we are as yet unable to comprehend how it acts, or to know its methods.''

Dr. Sheldon Leavitt, an American authority on the subconscious mind, has said: ''There is no disputing the fact that those who have given the subject of telepathy attentive thought and patient investigation have been convinced of its truth and practicability. My own experience has given me unwavering convictions. I know that in some way thought can be transmitted from one conscious mind to another; and I have good reason to believe that it can be transmitted still more forcibly and fully to the unconscious mind of the recipient.''

Camille Flammarion, the eminent French astronomer and scientist, says: ''One mind can act upon another at a distance without the habitual medium of words, or any other visible means of communication. It appears altogether unreasonable to reject this conclusion if we accept the facts. There is nothing unscientific, nothing romantic, in admitting that an idea can influence a brain from a distance. The action of one human being upon another, from a distance, is a scientific fact; it is as certain as the existence of Paris, of Napoleon, of Oxygen, or of Sirius. * * * There can be no doubt that our psychical force creates a movement of the ether, which transmits itself afar like all movements of ether, and becomes perceptible to brains in harmony with our own. The transformation of a psychic action into an ethereal movement, and the reverse, may be analogous to what takes place in a telephone, where the receptive plate, which is identical with the plate at the other end, reconstructs the sonorous movement transmitted, not by means of sound, but by electricity. But these are only comparisons.''

The student will notice that in the above quotations the scientific authorities dwell almost altogether upon the action of the **brain** as a receiving instrument. They have overlooked the equally important, and equally true fact that the organ-minds, the part-minds, the cell-minds, all the phases of the Corporeal Mind in fact, are capable of receiving the vibrations of the induced thought current, and of understanding them and of acting upon them. Were this not true, the phenomena of distant mental healing could not exist as it does at p   .

We have here a wonderfully interesting and important phase of the general subject of Mental Healing, and we should carefully acquaint ourselves with every phase of its activities and processes. I shall go into every phase in detail in the succeeding several lessons, and I ask every student to carefully consider what I have to say in those lessons. I shall deal not with theory alone, but shall go into the "just how" side of the subject.

R.

LESSON XIX

HOW THOUGHT TRAVELS TO A DISTANCE

In practicing Distant Thought Induction, the practitioner should proceed along the same general lines that I have laid down in the instructions regarding Personal Thought Induction; that is, at least, so far as is concerned the mental attitude to be preserved, the character of the thoughts and mental pictures to be held in his mind, and the character of silent mental suggestions, commands and instructions to be sent by him to the Corporeal Mind of the patient, or to his cell-minds, organ-minds, or part-minds. The only additional process necessary is **the establishing of mental lines of communication** between the practitioner and the mind of his patient. Let us then carefully study the nature and details of this process of mental line-building.

The first impression of students when they arrive at this stage of our instruction is that they are to be instructed how to build up some strange kind of telegraph system or lines, over which the mental currents shall travel. Now, this is a mistake, although a perfectly natural one—let us see in what the mistake lies, for by so doing we shall perceive the true state of affairs. Let us take our familiar analogy of electricity, for it will work out very well in this case as in the others we have already considered.

MENTAL THERAPEUTICS

While it is true that in the case of the passage of the electric current over the ordinary telegraph lines wires are employed, it is likewise true that in the case of electric **induction** the current does not pass over the conduction wires but rather leaps out of them and sets up a corresponding current in the neighboring conductor; likewise, in wireless telegraphy the current does not require wires to conduct it to its destination, but rather travels along **ethereal lines of its own making** until it reaches the receiving instrument which is attuned to it, and which has attracted it. In precisely the same ways Thought proceeds to its destination —its three ways of proceeding almost perfectly corresponding to those of electricity. For instance, Thought travels over the telegraph wires of the nervous system, and thus reaches each and . every part of the body of its manifestor, setting them into activity, and regulating their processes. Again, it leaps beyond the limits of the nervous system, and by induction sets up similar vibrations in the minds of those within its field of induction. And, finally, **it makes mental lines of its own** over which it proceeds to a distance, where it sets up similar vibrations in the mind of the person to whom it is directed, and who has attracted it. So you see, as I have said, the analogy to electricity is practically perfect.

In Distant Thought Induction the thought of the practitioner **actually builds up its own lines of communication** to the mind of the patient, and then travels over it. This **may** seem strange at first, for it is a natural question of the average student, "But how does it proceed at all when there are no lines or channels to carry it; how does it proceed to build its own lines and then travel over them; how does it get ahead of itself in order to build the lines over which it will travel later on?" These are legitimate and logical questions, and the student is perfectly justified in asking them. But the answer is equally logical and natural—it must be all of this, for it expresses an actual natural fact known to all advanced students of the subject. Here is the answer: **Thought projects from itself the lines over which it travels to a distance.** Let us see how this is.

You have heard of those wonderful "motor tractors" invented by the American manufacturers of agricultural machinery, and which are used to travel (and pull along after them certain things like plows, etc.) over fields too muddy and soft to bear the weight of ordinary wheels. These same wonderful instruments have been converted into those terrible gigantic armored machines, those traveling fortresses, which were invented by the British and used by them in the Great War in the year 1916, and which the soldiers called "the tanks." The distinctive principle of these machines is that of a great revolving track which the machine constantly unwinds and lays down in front of itself, and over which its real wheels then travel. While to read the description of this process sounds something like the recital of the efforts of a man to raise himself up into the air by his own bootstraps, nevertheless the process is in strict accordance with established mechanical laws, and it works out unfailingly. Well, this is a crude illustration of how both electricity and Thought lay their own lines before them, and then travel over them in wireless telegraphy and distant thought induction, respectively.

There is a point to be noted here, however, in the cases of both electricity and thought currents —the fact that both of these currents travel in **all directions** from the senders. But just as science has perfected methods by which the wireless current may be concentrated upon one focal point to a great extent, so has practical psychology perfected plans whereby thought currents may be concentrated upon one focal point, and directed to this point with increased force. And, we must note here also, in passing, that just as the receiving instrument of the wireless system "picks up" only those vibrations to which it has been attuned, so may the patient attune himself to the thought vibrations of the practitioner, and thus more readily "pick up" his own special message.

Then, the students ask, how do we proceed to start into activity this process whereby the mental track is laid over which our thought currents are to flow to the patient? The answer is simple: **You build the track, or mental path, by thinking of it.** The simple process of Creative Thought itself performs the work of building the track, or laying down the line over which your thought vibrations shall travel. We perform this work unconsciously every day of our lives, when we think intently of a person; though in such cases there is seldom the degree of strength manifested which accompanies conscious deliberate efforts in this direction—there is usually lacking that concentration which produces forceful and effective results in the work of thought transmission.

The practitioner, in order to get the best results, should first establish a strong, clear, unobstructed line of mental communication with the patient; this will remain after the treatment, and will render easier the subsequent treatments —though it will be found well to keep the line in order, the track clear, by a little attention each day or so. This direct mental line or track is built by the practitioner simply **thinking it into existence**—by visualizing it as in existence, by creating a mental picture of it as actually in existence. There is no need of going into the metaphysical or occult explanation of this wonderful phenomenon—for such would take us far away from our present subject, and would involve us in a mass of technical instruction which is entirely foreign to the purposes of the present work; it is enough to know that this process "works out," and is scientifically correct.

The more vivid the practitioner can make this mental track or path between himself and the patient—the clearer he can visualize it in his "mind's eye," the more effective will be the currents that travel over it, and the closer the "en rapport" condition between the patient and himself. If he can instruct **the patient** to aid in this work of path-building there will, of course, be a much greater degree of "en rapport" condition existing between them—a **mental agreement** naturally always produces better results in these cases.

The practitioner will find that it will help him materially in this work of building up a mental path for the purpose of Distant Healing, if he will form a clear mental picture of the patient at a distance, and will direct his thought of track-building toward him or her when he is establishing the "en rapport" condition. It is not necessary to visualize the actual appearance of the patient, for that is often impossible in cases where the patient is not personally known to the healer; it is sufficient that a general mental image of **a person named So-and-So** is seen in the distance, and the mental track be built toward that person. So we healers deny the necessity of this preliminary work, but a little close questioning will usually bring to light the fact that they actually do this work more or less unconsciously; they have trained themselves to quick work along these lines, and so they actually build the track while they are thinking of the patient. It is an invariable rule of thought transmission, that the vibrations always travel over a path or track—and that this track has to be built, consciously or unconsciously.

Occultists have for thousands of years been **aware of the efficacy** of that which has been called "The Astral Tube" in the process of distant thought transmission—and the principle has been employed to advantage by many of the world's best distant healers, although others have preferred their own methods which in the end bring into effect the same general principles. The Astral Tube is created and used in the following manner:

The Astral Tube. What occultists call the Astral Tube consists of the building up on the astral plane (the plane next above the physical plane of being), of a tube or tunnel which acts as a most effective channel for the transmission of thought currents or thought vibrations. It is created entirely by the creative power of the mind, and depends for its strength and permanency upon the clearness and power of the visualization, or mental picturing, of the mind of the person creating it.

The Astral Tube is created by the person first shutting from his mind all disturbing influences, and then concentrating upon the task of creating the image in the astral substance. He begins by gazing in the general direction of the person between whom and himself he wishes to build the tube. Then he pictures in his mind a great cloud of smoke-like substance filling the space between them. Then he mentally **pierces** that volume of astral vapor, by setting up **a whirling motion in its center.** Then he pictures this whirling motion proceeding like a miniature cyclone, boring its way rapidly through the volume of smoke-like substance, and thus creating a tunnel-like bore, tube, or circular opening through its entire extent, until finally appearing at the other end is perceived the figure of the person thought of. The subsequent opening up of this psychic channel is comparatively easy—much easier than the first work of course.

Remember that, in the words of the average person, this work is **all in the imagination**—the Creative Imagination, however, as all occultists know, is not a thing of mere fancy, but is rather a most powerful creative agency on the astral plane. And astral plane phenomena are, in their own field, as real and actual as are the phenomena of the material plane in their own field.

And now, having mastered the theory of Distant Induction, and the fundamental principles of its practice, let us proceed to the consideration of the details of its practice in the work of actual healing. We are dealing with a fascinating subject, and are naturally impatient at too much delay in getting to the point of manifestation.

LESSON XX

HOW TO HEAL AT A DISTANCE

In preparing the patient for your distant healing currents, he should be instructed to place himself in a receptive mental attitude toward such treatments. He should be taught to mentally open himself to the inflow of your healing thought currents, and to assume the mental attitude of perfect willingness to receive such inflow. This removes the friction which the subconscious mind sometimes sets up to thought currents from outside (a very wise provision of nature, by the way), and renders your work much easier and much more effective. You should, of course, caution the patient against making himself receptive to all thought currents from outside; **he should be taught to make the mental statement that he is passive to your thoughts only, and resistive to all others which he does not wish to receive.**

Some patients like to be treated at a certain hour, and in such case it is well to fall in with their wishes, if the hour is convenient to you. But, inasmuch as this is not at all necessary for the success of the treatment, many of the best practitioners refuse to set or observe hours of treatment, and instead give the treatment at such times as are most convenient to them. The Corporeal Mind of the patient is always wide awake—always "at home"—even when his conscious mind is wrapped in sleep; so that it may

161

be reached at any time with equal effect. The patient may be informed of this, and told that all that is necessary is to take the general mental attitude **that your healing thought currents are always welcome.**

When the time for the treatment has arrived, you should strengthen and make clear the mental path or line which you have erected, and thus firmly establish the en rapport condition. This you do by sitting quietly and **thinking the line clear,** in the way I have already described to you. A little practice will soon **inform** you just when the desired condition is reached; at such times there comes to the practitioner a peculiar feeling of **closeness** to the patient—a strange sense of the two persons being in the actual presence of each other. When you experience this feeling fully, then you will know that the conditions are favorable for the treatment. If you experience difficulty in securing these conditions, do not become worried, impatient, or discouraged, for a little patient, calm concentration will soon bring about the desired result.

When you are satisfied that the best possible conditions have been secured, and the best possible degree of en rapport established, then you should proceed to **visualize or mentally picture the patient as present in the same room with you.** Forget all about the mental wires, paths, or tracks, or astral tubes (for the time being), for you have already established the connection, and your thought process will subconsciously keep the line open until the treatment is completed. **In imagination, see your patient as standing or seated before you** (whichever you prefer). Throw yourself as thoroughly as possible into the idea of this direct presence, for it is a most potent factor in these distant treatments. Do not waste time in trying to picture the features of the person, for indeed you may not know these—it is sufficient that you imagine a Somebody present before you, that Somebody being your patient of course. From this point proceed precisely as if you were giving the treatment of Mental Suggestion, or Personal Thought Induction, or a combination of both. Speak, aloud, or in a whisper, to the patient before you, if you wish; or if you prefer you may direct to him your silent mental suggestions, instruction, or commands. **In every way act exactly as if he were actually before you in person**—for from the occult viewpoint he is actually so, your en rapport condition bringing you actually in mental contact with him.

From this point, you are to proceed simply as you would in the case of a patient who had called upon you in person for treatment. Hold the same mental picture of the patient manifesting perfect health; give the same mental instructions to the Corporeal Mind, and to the cell-minds or organ-minds, as you would in personal treatment by any method we have studied and considered. So true is this that many of the best distant healers actually address the distant patient with the greeting of "Good Morning," or "How do you do, Mr. Smith; sit down and rest yourself a few moments before we begin our treatment;" and actually bid them "Good-bye," or "Good Morning" after the treatment is over. This may seem like fantastic nonsense—but when you have tried it a few times you will see how natural it comes to you, and how effective it is. Do not dismiss anything contained in these lessons, until you have given it a fair and unprejudiced trial; all of the things regarding which you are being instructed in these lessons are the result of the actual experience of many of the world's best healers, and as such demand at least respectful consideration and a fair trial from you or any other student who wishes to attain scientific knowledge of this great subject.

I shall now give you a practical example of Distant Healing, along the general lines just set down for you. I have taken as an example a case which is quite common in the practice of all practitioners—you will recognize it often when you get into actual practice, so you will do well to fix its general principles in your memory. It is a case of general "run down health," arising from imperfect nutrition and poor elimination, which has resulted in weakness, poor blood supply, cold hands and feet, impaired sense of smell, hearing, and taste, poor memory, and dizziness in the head, etc. When you meet these cases in person, you easily recognize them by their pallor, thinness, cold hands, and general appearance; likewise you recognize the general symptoms when they write to you telling their troubles. Drug treatment does little or nothing for these patients, and they soon develop into chronic cases—but the right kind of Mental Healing treatment soon works an improvement upon them, and if kept up nearly always results in a cure. You will notice that the treatment goes right to the spot, and is directed along the lines of scientific physiology plus scientific psychology.

Typical Case. Having established the en rapport condition between the patient and yourself, you **create the mental picture or visualization of the patient as being actually present in the room with you.** This being secured, you proceed to address the patient just as you would in the case of ordinary personal presence, viz.: "Good morning, Mrs. Smith, I am glad to see you. You are looking better this morning—you know that you are going to get better, going to be perfectly well pretty soon, don't you? Of course you do; and that is just what is going to happen to you—you are going to get better at once, and then still better, and then better still; and so on better and better each day, until in a short time we will have you all right again, enjoying better health than you ever did in your life; all your troubles gone and forgotten, and you so happy and well and strong that you will seem like another woman. That is what this treatment is going to do for you, Mrs. Smith— and away down in your heart you realize it, do you not? Of course you do—you know it intuitively, and that's just why you are here this morning; here to be cured and made well!

"Mrs. Smith, I now see you as a strong, healthy woman. I see you before me as nature intended you to be, and as you really are in Truth. You have plumped out, your cheeks are rosy and your lips red, your eyes are bright and your skin soft and pleasant to the touch. I can see into your body, and there I perceive all of your organs functioning properly, and busily engaged in their work of building up a strong and well body, and keeping it in that condition. Every part of your body is doing its work properly; every organ is functioning properly; every cell is doing its work splendidly, just as nature intended it to do. You have a strong, healthy body, doing its work properly, and that is why I see you before me as an ideal Healthy Woman. And, oh, how happy you seem to be well and strong once more.

"I see that your digestive organs are working splendidly, and are digesting and assimilating every bit of nourishment in the food you eat. Consequently, you have a good natural appetite for normal healthy food—even a crust of dry bread tastes good to you, for when you chew it you realize that you are extracting nourishment from it which is going to strengthen you and keep you strong. Your food is being transmuted into rich red blood which is coursing through your veins and building up every part of your body and strengthening it. Your brain is well nourished, and this keeps your senses in good working order. You hear well, taste well, smell well, see well, and feel well—your sense organs are all working properly, because they are well nourished. Your hands and feet are warm, for there is plenty of blood going to them and nourishing them. Your head is clear and your memory is good, because your brain is now well nourished.

"Your organs of elimination are working beautifully, and are throwing out of the system all the waste matter and impurities that nature wishes to discard. Your bowels are working finely; you have a natural movement of the bowels once a day, at the time you set for it—and you always keep your engagement with your bowels, for you have promised to act well by them if they act well by you, and you are both keeping your contract. Your reproductive organs are in perfect condition, and you have no trouble whatever from them. Your menstruation is regular and normal, and free from pain, for you have established a new order of things in your general care of the body, and all of the various parts and organs are responding properly thereto.

"You are bright, cheerful and happy all the time, all the day, and everywhere. You take an interest in life, and see everything as a new and happy world. You take an interest in what is going on about you, and are thus keeping young and active. You feel the spirit of Youth bubbling in you, and you are enjoying Life anew."

Here you should give specific suggestions to

the various organs of the body above referred to, or which may be reported as in trouble; you speak to them just as if they were separate entities, according to the principles explained to you in preceding lessons of this course. It makes no difference that the patient is distant in space from you—the principle is precisely the same as I have explained to you. In some cases you will get better results from the "general treatment" as above described; in others, you will get much better results from the organ-mind or cell-mind treatment; therefore, it is always better to try both in order to gain the benefit of both methods.

You should terminate the treatment with bidding the patient good-bye, and giving her a strong, hopeful suggestion or statement that she will find herself feeling better each hour, and that she will feel like another woman by the time of the next treatment. **Remember, that all your statements and suggestions reach the Corporeal Mind of the patient; and the organ-minds and cell-minds as well.** Like a little child listening quietly in a room, the Corporeal Mind of the patient is eagerly listening to every word of your treatment—therefore be sure to get in the right kind of suggestions and statements, that they may take form in physical states and conditions.

LESSON XXI

THE PHYSIOLOGY OF MENTAL HEALING

In the earlier lessons of this course, I explained to you that all Mental Healing is really the effect of Mind over minds—of the higher Mind over the minds in the organs, parts, and cells of the body. When this fact and principle is once grasped by the student, he begins to realize that the work of healing must be directed to the cell-minds and organ-minds, either directly or else through the Corporeal Mind which is but the sum-total of these subordinate cell-minds and organ-minds. And he likewise realizes that the most effective mental treatment must be along the lines of inducing normal activities in the organs and cells. While a general appeal and course of energizing suggestions directed to the Corporeal Mind generally acts in the direction of cure, and often is all that is needed; nevertheless scientific practice should include specific and special direction of the treatment to the particular organ, part, or cells which are manifesting imperfectly.

The student also grasps the idea that his treatment must not be along negative lines—that it must not consist of thoughts and words about the diseased conditions; but rather it should be expressly and invariably along positive and constructive lines; that is, it must consist of thoughts and words about the normal, natural, healthy condition of the organ or part affected.

169

MENTAL THERAPEUTICS

The thought of the practitioner, and his every word and suggestion, must be along the lines of **the condition he wishes to produce in the patient. He must always see and think of the desired condition as already existing.**

But (and here we come to a most important question) how is the practitioner to picture and treat for the normal, natural, healthy condition **unless he knows just what these healthy, normal, natural conditions really are?** The answer is obvious—there is no need of further argument about it. The answer is simply **"He cannot!"** This being so, I have deemed it advisable to include in these lessons, just as I do in my personal class lessons, a simple, plain, non-technical, clear presentation of the basic and fundamental facts of physiology—the facts of the natural and normal processes of the physical organs of a man or woman in the state of health. Those who have an acquaintance with this subject already will be none the worse for refreshing their memory; and those who have not an acquaintance therewith will be greatly benefited by a careful study of the following lessons in which these things are pointed out.

The student will notice, however, that in such instruction I shall not dwell upon the diseased conditions of the parts or organs, excepting perhaps here and there a passing reference thereto. My plan is entirely different from that of the teacher of drug-healing, who keeps the minds and thoughts of his students always on the diseased condition and never on the healthy condition. Is it any wonder that so many physicians grow morbid on the subject of disease—particularly the subject of the special class of diseases upon which they specialize? Is it any wonder that they are always looking for symptoms of their favorite disease, and always imagining that they find it? In view of what we know of the effect of mental images upon the physical states and conditions, it is no wonder that so many of these disease-specialists finally fall victims to their own favorite diseases—it would indeed be wonderful if such were not the case, in view of the known facts of psychological influence over the organ-minds and cell-minds. And, alas! it is also to be feared that in many cases the mental attitudes and mental images of these specialists actually induce corresponding diseased conditions in the bodies of the patients under their care. A simple understanding of the laws of mental suggestion should be sufficient to show the reasonableness of this suspicion.

So I have pursued an entirely opposite policy in these lessons. Instead of following the method of the orthodox teachers of medicine who, as an authority has well said, "stick to the old materialistic ideas and cultivate the thoughts engendered by close association with cadavers, morbid specimens, bacterial cultures, microscopic slides, and pathology in general," I have adopted the plan of pointing out to my students the Healthy, Natural, Normal Human Body; bidding them **always to hold this in their minds**

as a pattern to be used in building up a like condition in the bodies of their patients. This may seem like a small thing to those who do not look beneath the surface of things—but to those who look beneath the superficial appearance of things the fact is a most significant one, and one of the greatest importance in the practice of Mental Healing.

I have found that very many students at first have failed to recognize the great importance of the normal processes of that which we call "Nature," as manifested in the human body. Many have in a general way thought of Nature as merely a totality of mechanical forces, which operated by action and reaction, relation and interrelation, and general co-ordination, which have caused the "happening" of the processes of the physical body. This is a grave error of judgment, and important results may depend upon its correction. If it were merely a question of philosophy or general belief, I should not stop to speak of it here. But inasmuch as the success of the practitioner of Mental Therapeutics depends materially upon his conception of the activities underlying the processes of Nature, I deem it of the highest importance that students of the subject be correctly informed regarding this question.

Nature is not a totality of blind, lifeless forces. On the contrary, all **Nature is alive,** and is permeated with Mind in every part. There is nothing lifeless or mindless in all of Nature. Without attempting to explain the almost inconceivable mystery of Nature's operations, I wish to be understood as positively asserting that the processes manifested in the physical body of every human being in a state of health show the presence of **instinctive mind working toward the end of efficient work.** More than this, the human body as it exists today is the result of long ages of evolution, of efforts on the part of this instinctive mind to manifest better and still better results. Disease results from some interference with Nature's laws. If Nature in the body can have her own way, unhindered by external forces, she will build up and maintain a perfectly healthy physical system—for her aim and ideal always is Perfect Health.

One thing that the practitioner may always count upon in his treatments, and that is that Nature is always on his side in his healing work. Nature has as her twofold purpose (a) the preservation and well-being of the life of the individual, and (b) the reproduction and survival of the species. She is constantly working toward those ends. When she is thwarted in her ends she makes the best of it, and does the best she can in view of the imperfect material with which she has to work and the obstacles interfering with her full expression and manifestation. Away down in the depths of the Corporeal Mind will be found this primitive and elementary urge of Nature toward Perfect Health.

It may be urged that Nature kills a man as well as bringing him into life. This is true in a way, but it remains true that while man is in the limits of his natural years of life, Nature is always striving to keep him in health and strength. She intends that every man shall live out his normal period of time, and she intends that he shall live it in health and strength. If Nature's laws were not interfered with, disease and short-life would be but as accidents.

· So truly does Nature work always in the interests of health and life, that even many conditions called "disease" are but Nature's remedial processes—processes designed to cast from the system that which is harmful to it. Nearly all acute disease is really a remedial process, when rightly understood. But when Nature is unable to accomplish her work, she apparently resigns herself to the task of making the best of it, and the limits of his natural years of life, Nature is always striving to keep him in health and strength. She intends that every man shall live out his normal period of time, and she intends that he shall live it in health and strength. If Nature's laws were not interfered with, disease and short-life would be but as accidents.

· So truly does Nature work always in the interests of health and life, that even many conditions called "disease" are but Nature's remedial processes—processes designed to cast from the system that which is harmful to it. Nearly all acute disease is really a remedial process, when rightly understood. But when Nature is unable to accomplish her work, she apparently resigns herself to the task of making the best of it, and struggles along in a halting and limping fashion —this allows the diseased condition to become "chronic." In our treatments we really help Nature by imparting energy and activity to the cell-minds and organ-minds, and thus throwing off the abnormal conditions. **All healing consists in restoring Nature's normal rule and operations.**

All this leads up to what I shall have to say to you in the succeeding lessons of this course, in which I shall show you Nature in normal action—her processes performed in the natural, normal way which maintain physical health and well-being. Any deviation from this normal standard of operations means ill-health or disease. The closer you study the conditions maintained by Nature when the body is in a state of

PHYSIOLOGY OF MENTAL HEALING

Perfect Health, the better able will you be to direct your thought, suggestions, and other suggestions, and other treatment to the best effect.

General Directions: I wish here to give you certain general directions regarding the study of the following lessons, and the application of the principles therein contained:

(1) Take up each lesson in turn, and carefully study the principles of Nature's operations as manifested in the particular department treated upon in the lesson. Do not leave the lesson until you have formed a clear, general idea of the operations of Nature in that particular office and function, or class of the same. Go back to the subject over and over again until you have mastered it completely. It may help you in your study if you will write down a short synopsis of each lesson, without reference to the book during the writing—use your own words and ways of stating the principle. Then compare what you have written with the lesson itself, and note your mistakes and omissions. Stick to it until you have a very clear idea of the subject in your mind; so clear that you may easily describe it to a friend in conversation.

(2) When you have gained a clear idea of the subject of the lesson, in fact even while you are gaining it, you should practice **visualizing** or forming a clear mental picture in your imagination of the process you have been studying. Try to picture it just as you would if you were actually viewing the process in a human body,

if this were possible. I want you to be able to picture these leading physiological processes just as clearly as you would picture the workings of a piece of familiar machinery—the running of a train, a typewriter, or a sewing-machine, for instance.

(3) When you come to actual practice, I want you to reproduce the idea and mental picture of this normal, natural, functioning of the organs in question, so that you may actually picture the corresponding organs of the patient as acting in the same way. By doing this you actually set up processes in the body of the patient which will bring about just this kind of activity and normal functioning. Do you get the point? By creating the correct mental pattern in your mind, and then reproducing it in connection with your thought of the patient's body, you tend to make the ideal pattern take on objective form and activity in the patient's system. Do you see now why I dwell so strongly upon the necessity of your creating the right kind of mental pattern? To this end the instruction given in the following lessons has been written.

LESSON XXII

THE NUTRITIVE PROCESSES

First of all of the important processes of Nature in her work of building-up, repairing and sustaining the human body, are the processes of Nutrition. The processes of Nutrition are those by which the normal condition of life and growth of the living organism is maintained, and which operate in the direction of the living tissues of the body **taking up from the blood** the nourishing materials or substances required for their repair and the performance of their healthy functions.

You will note the following two facts: (1) That the tissues take up nourishing material or substance in order that they may keep in repair and perform their ˙healthy functions—**this nourishment is food, and the products of food;** and (2) that **this nourishment is taken up from the blood.** We have here two great facts of physical life, viz.: (a) That the tissues require and take up FOOD; and (b) that this food is obtained from the BLOOD, and the blood only. (By "the tissues" physiologists mean the material and substance of the organs, muscles, etc., composing the physical body.) Now then, the next thing to ascertain (1) **how this nourishment gets into the blood;** and (2) how it is extracted and taken up from the blood by the tissues.

Let us begin at the beginning. The food of the human being, composed of animal or vegetable substance, is taken into the mouth, where it is broken up into bits so as to be more easily digested a little later on. But in the mouth we also find the first steps or processes of digestion performed. There are located in the mouth six important glands known as the **salivary glands;** four of these are located under the tongue and jaw, and two in the cheeks in front of the ears. These glands manufacture and give forth through numerous ducts a fluid substance called "saliva," more commonly known as "spittle." Mixing with the food, while the latter is being chewed, the saliva performs the chemical process of converting the starchy portion of the food into sugar or glucose, and thus performing the first stage of its assimilation into the system. This chemical process is continued as the food passes down the gullet, but practically ceases when the stomach is reached. (In cases of indigestion, it is well to give some little attention to the cells composing these glands, in your general treatment, for it often happens that they are more or less inactive.)

The stomach is the great chemical laboratory of the body, and in it are performed many important chemical processes in the direction of converting the food-mass into the ultimate form of nourishment in which it is taken up by the blood. In the stomach is manufactured, by countless minute glands, that strong digestive fluid known as "the gastric juice." This juice is a very powerful chemical substance which acts as a solvent upon the nitrogenous portions of the food, and also upon the sugar or glucose into which the starches of the food have been converted by the saliva. One of its most active ingredients is that known as **pepsin**, which is a powerful digestive agent. About one gallon of gastric juice is manufactured by the healthy stomach each twenty-four hours. It is mixed up with the food very thoroughly by a peculiar churning motion of the stomach which tosses and kneads the food-mass so that the gastric juice is well mixed up with every particle of it, and thus able to perform its chemical processes.

If this work of digestion in the stomach is not performed for any reason, as, for instance, the stomach having been weakened by abuse and over work, or by the placing into it of too much indigestible stuff, then **fermentation** is apt to result, and the food-mass, instead of being digested properly, is converted into a putrefying, rotting, yeasty mass, which instead of nourishing the blood practically poisons it. In such cases we have dyspepsia and other diseases resulting from imperfect digestion and assimilation. In such cases the stomach and its glands should be specifically treated by the practitioner, and encouraged to perform their work properly. The stomach, as I have said elsewhere in these lessons, is a very obedient organ—something like a big, gentle, intelligent Newfoundland dog so far as its mentality is concerned. By proper treatment it may be encouraged to resume normal and natural functioning; but the patient should be told to treat it properly in return. In treating the stomach, address yourself not only to it in itself, but also to the glands manufacturing the gastric juice—it is astonishing how these glands will respond to an earnest appeal, and will manufacture a sufficient amount of gastric juice with a sufficient amount of pepsin in it to do the work properly. Treatment of this kind just before a meal will often give the patient a keen appetite, and will result in perfect digestion of that meal. The experiment is most interesting and instructive.

After the food-mass has been treated by and in the stomach as I have just described, it is passed on and out of the stomach on the right-hand side, and enters into what is known as the Small Intestine. The Small Intestine is a long tube, entrail or gut, which is from twenty to thirty feet in length, but which is so ingeniously coiled upon itself as to occupy but a comparatively small space in the body—this intestine must not be confused with the Colon or large intestine which carries away the refuse or garbage of the system to be discharged from the body. The Small Intestine is an important part of the main organs of nutrition. Its surface is lined with a velvety substance which brushes against the food-mass which passes along it, and acts to absorb the fluid food-substance when properly digested.

When the food-mass enters the Small Intestine it is met with a strong, peculiar fluid called Bile, which becomes thoroughly mixed up with it and worked into it. The Bile is manufactured by the Liver to the extent of about two quarts a day, and is stored up for future use in what is called the Gall-Bladder. There is also poured into the food in this stage another strong fluid, called the Pancreatic Juice, which is manufactured to the extent of about one and one-half pints daily by the Pancreas, or "sweetbread," an organ situated just behind the stomach. The work of the Bile and the Pancreatic Juice is to act upon the fatty portions of the food-mass so as to render it capable of being absorbed into the blood; the Bile also acts to prevent decomposition and putrefaction of the food as it passes through the intestine, and also to neutralize the gastric juice which has already performed its work and is no longer needed by the system.

In cases of digestive trouble, the practitioner should always treat the Small Intestine, the Pancreas, and the Liver. The first two organs are, like the stomach, quite receptive and responsive to mental treatment—in fact, they are rather more gentle than even that organ, and rather resemble the intelligent well-bred hunting-dog in their mental character. The Liver, on the contrary, as I have said before, is stubborn, rather stupid, and "heavy" in its mentality —it is like the pig or the mule, and must be treated vigorously, firmly, and positively, and emphatically told that it must get to work properly and efficiently.

The food-mass in the Small Intestine is a soft, semi-liquid substance produced by the process of digestion of the food originally taken into the mouth. It reaches the Small Intestine from the stomach in the form of a pasty substance called Chyme. This Chyme is transformed by the intestinal juices and Bile into three derivative substances, namely: (1) Peptone, derived from the digestion of albuminous substances; (2) Chyle, derived from the emulsion of the fatty substances; and (3) Glucose, derived from the transformation of the starchy substances. It should be noted, however, that the fluids taken into the stomach as drink, as well as the fluids liberated from the solids in the process of digestion in the stomach, do not reach the Small Intestine at all—instead, they are rapidly taken up by the absorbent apparatus of the stomach and carried into the blood, and thence to the kidneys and bladder, and finally voided from the system in the urine. Some of the fluids, of course, are retained in the body to perform necessary work therein.

The work of absorption of the digested food substances, or nourishment, from the Small Intestine into the blood is performed by the millions of plush-like "hairs" of the velvety inner surface of the Small Intestine, which maintain a constant waving motion through the semi-liquid digested food contained therein, and "lick up" and absorb the nourishment now fitted for the system. In this way the Peptone and Glucose are carried into the blood to the Liver, and then passed through the heart as you shall learn in a later lesson. The Chyle is absorbed by the lymphatic vessels called "the lacteals," and thence to the thoracic duct, and then gradually conveyed to the blood.

In a subsequent lesson I shall take up the story of the assimilation of the food from this point, and show you the processes whereby the blood carries this nourishment to all parts of the body, nourishing cells and tissue, organs and parts, building-up and repairing each. To many it seems a strange idea that the blood is the carrier and distributor of this nourishment derived from the food—but it is a scientific fact nevertheless.

In another subsequent lesson I shall take up the subject of the elimination of the waste products which remain after the nourishment is extracted from the food by the processes of digestion.

Before passing on, however, I wish to impress upon the minds of students and practitioners the fact that in most cases of chronic ailments the original cause of the trouble is to be found in these main organs of nutrition. If the body is not sufficiently nourished, or if it be furnished with improper material, it is bound to rebel and manifest in the form of abnormal function or disease. No matter what may be the superficial symptoms, it will always be well to take these organs into account, and to give them the proper treatment. In fact, many of the best practitioners, before proceeding to more local treatment, give a strong, thorough, preliminary treatment both to the main organs of nutrition and the organs of elimination. If the body is properly nourished, and its waste products are properly carried off, the liability of disease is materially lessened, and the work of cure rendered materially easier and simpler.

The body has often been compared to a piece of intricate machinery, which is run by the steam of the vital force. This steam is generated by the fires of the furnace of the organs of nutrition; and these fires must be kept well supplied with the nourishment of the proper kind of food, and fanned by the draft of perfect functioning. Also, the ashes and clinkers must not be allowed to accumulate—the work of the organs of elimination must be kept normal, and up to the mark.

Hence, student and practitioners, keep these two main points always before you—**attend well to the organs of nutrition, and those of elimination, and nine-tenths of your work is accomplished.** For, from imperfect digestion and assimilation, and imperfect elimination, arise a veritable swarm of diseases, symptoms, and physical troubles.

LESSON XXIII

THE ELIMINATIVE PROCESSES

Second in importance only to the nutritive processes of the body are its eliminative processes. And some would deny even this relegation of the latter to second place, for they plausibly maintain that no matter how well the body may be nourished it will not remain in a state of health if it is unable to eliminate properly its waste products, its debris, its garbage.

The word "eliminate" means "to put out, to expel, to discharge." The body eliminates its waste matter and products in four ways, viz.: (1) Through the breath; (2) through the skin, in the perspiration; (3) through the kidneys, in the urine; and (4) through the bowels, in the fæces or excrement.

In a later lesson I shall describe the process of elimination through the breath, in which the waste products of the system, carried in the blood to the lungs, are there consumed by the oxygen in the air breathed into the lungs, and expelled in the form of carbonic acid gas.

Elimination through the skin, by means of the perspiration, is a far more important process than is realized by the average person. There are over three million sweat glands in the human body, the combined length of the secreting tubes being about two or three miles. The normal adult human being excretes about one and one-half pint to two pints of perspiration every twenty-four hours, that amount of course being greatly exceeded by men doing manual work in hot places, such as rolling mills, engine rooms, etc. Sweat or perspiration is seen by chemical analysis to be loaded with the refuse matter of the system, it being in fact but little different from the urine in its chemical composition. The excretory glands of the skin are really supplementary organs to the kidneys, and in case of kidney troubles they perform a great deal of the work that ordinarily falls to the lot of the kidneys.

The kidneys are two organs located in the loins, behind the intestines, one on each side of the spinal column. They are shaped like a bean, and are about four inches long, two inches wide, and one inch thick. Their office is to purify the blood by extracting from it a poisonous substance called urea, and certain other waste products of the system, which would cause blood poisoning if not eliminated from the system. The watery fluid secreted by the kidneys is called **urine,** and is carried from the kidneys to the bladder, in which organ it is stored up to be afterwards voided from the body in the process of urination.

"The bowels" is a term commonly employed to indicate the Large Intestine, or Colon, into which the undigested food, and discarded material of food, is passed from the Small Intestine; and through which it passes in the process of elimination or excretion which ends in **its** discharge from the body in the act of evacuation, "stool," or "movement." The Colon (large intestine, or "large bowel") is a large tubular gut or intestine nearly five feet in length, which passes up from the lower right-hand side of the abdomen, then across the abdomen to the upper left-hand side, then down along the left-hand side to its lower portion; at the last mentioned point it makes a twist or curve, and then grows smaller, and finally ends in the rectum or exit from the system, its termination being the **anus** or posterior opening through which the excrement is expelled in the "movement" or stool.

The Small Intestine empties its discarded matter into the Colon by a curious little trapdoor arrangement on the lower right-hand side of the abdomen—the **V**ermiform Appendix being situated just below this entrance. The waste matter or fæces then rises slowly up the right-hand side of the Colon; then along its horizontal length, which extends across the abdomen; then down the left-hand side of the Colon, into the curve or twist called the Sigmoid Flexure, and then into the rectum, and finally out through the anus. Its movement along the length of the Colon is caused by certain muscular movements provided for that purpose.

The Colon is **the great sewer of the system,** which Nature has provided for the carrying off of the waste products resulting from undigested or undigestible portions of food, and other waste products of the system. Nature intended that this sewerage should be removed speedily, and in the case of animals and young children it is so removed. But the artificial habits and customs of adult human beings has sadly interfered with this natural and normal custom, and bad results have ensued for the race. But Nature accommodates herself to circumstances, as we have seen elsewhere in the lessons; and if man would only carry out a settled plan of preparing for a movement of the bowels each day, and adhering to his resolve to give Nature a chance to do this work for him, he would manage to get along with practically no trouble on this score. But he will not even do this. He refuses to heed Nature's calls, until at last Nature (and by Nature here is meant the Bowel-Mind) becomes discouraged and does as little as she can help—and the result is chronic constipation with all of its attendant evils.

Let me point out to you the results of this unnatural state of affairs. In the first place the inner walls of the Colon become incrusted with impacted fæcal matter, some of it remaining there for many days, its fluids becoming absorbed until the remaining mass becomes quite hard and tightly packed together. A small hole is worked through this hardened mass, through which a small quantity of excrement is passed. The Colon so impacted and incrusted becomes a source of danger to the general system—it is like a choked up sewer flowing through a city. The fluid portion is absorbed into the blood through the walls of the intestine, and thus tends to poison the blood and all the parts of the body.

THE ELIMINATIVE PROCESSES

This state of affairs is manifested by foul breath, strong perspiration, and strong urine—these resulting from Nature's efforts to get rid of the foul matter by some other route. Dyspepsia, billiousness, liver troubles, kidney troubles, rheumatism, nervousness and many other ailments arise from this state of affairs. Many cases of female trouble are caused by the pressure of the impacted Colon upon the generative organs, and by the poisoning of the latter by reason of their nearness to the foul sewer of the Colon.

The practitioner will discover that when he removes the causes of constipation, and thus takes away the original cause of the troubles above alluded to, the symptoms of many of these diseases will disappear. In fact, many of the best practitioners now proceed to first treat all their patients for imperfect elimination, and by so doing they remove the original causes of the particular diseases for which they have sought treatment. The patient may easily determine whether or not his or her Colon is in this abnormal condition by an examination of the color of the stool or movement. The waste matter or fæces when first passed into the Colon from the small intestine is of a pasty consistency, and a light color; if the bowels operate naturally the fæces is discharged from the rectum in a soft state and of a light yellow color. The longer it remains in the Colon the darker it gets in color, and the harder in consistency. Fæces in a Colon which is very much incrusted often appears as a hard lump of a dark green color. These facts make the diagnosis easy.

The practitioner will find that the Colon, as well as the Kidneys, are quite receptive and amenable to suggestion, either given verbally or mentally, either in present treatment or distant treatment. The Kidneys may be instructed to work more freely, or else to refrain from excessive work as the case may be. The **normal condition** should always be the pattern held in mind, and upon which the treatment is modelled. The Colon will respond quite readily to mental treatment having for its purpose the removal of Constipation. It will be found that the Colon actually seems to be fully aware of the existing state of affairs, and is anxious to have normal activity restored. But it has been so long neglected, and its calls and requests so persistently refused and denied, that it has lost interest, courage and activity, and has relapsed into a state of apathy. It has acquired bad habits, and its cells and muscles have been weakened by disuse.

In treating for Constipation, there are two things to be remembered, as follows: (1) The treatment of the Colon itself, in the direction of bidding it "brace up" and regain its normal natural energy; and also to at once start in to acquire the habit of manifesting **one movement a day,** regularly and invariably. It must be thoroughly drilled and impressed with this idea, over and over again, until you have awakened in it its original activities, and have set into motion in it the vibrations which will raise it up to normal functioning. And (2) you must impress upon your patient (by word or by letter) the importance of this condition being removed—the common sense of most patients will grasp the underlying theory of this matter if it is presented to them properly. The patient should be instructed to fix in mind a certain hour of the day when it will be most convenient to go to the closet, and then to keep in mind that hour, and to regard it as **a positive engagement.** When the hour arrives the patient should retire to the closet, in order to keep the engagement, even though he have not the slightest call of Nature in that direction. This should be faithfully carried out each day, until the new habit has been fixed. This course will result in establishing the normal and natural habit of bowel-evacuation. Your treatments should, of course, be along the same lines—that of normal, natural, regular habits of bowel-evacuation. If you observe the above stated general principles and practice you should be able to cure cases of chronic constipation which have defied the efforts of the best drug practitioners.

In addition to the above methods of treating constipation, it will be well for you to encourage the patient to drink more water each day. The normal amount of water called for by the system is about two quarts in twenty-four hours on an average. But very few persons ever keep up to this standard—some fall far below it. Now, this is not advising your patient to take water as a **remedy** or medicine, any more than the use of food can be considered a remedy for malnutrition. The facts of the case are that unless the system is given sufficient fluids to work with, it cannot carry on its processes naturally and normally, no matter how efficient its organs may be. Water is needed to absorb and carry off the waste products of the system in the blood, in the breath, in the perspiration, in the urine, and in the fæces carried off by the bowels. The mental healer should not attempt to ignore the plain facts of physiology in his enthusiasm regarding the Power of the Mind; instead he should adapt his treatment to existing facts of physiology. He should fall in with Nature's ways, instead of trying to run contrary to them. For in the end Nature performs the cures—and Nature is the Corporeal Mind and its subordinate phases and forms.

LESSON XXIV

"THE BLOOD IS THE LIFE"

Although the discovery of the circulation of the blood is of comparatively recent date, yet from the earliest times thoughtful men have recognized the all-important offices of the blood in the vital processes. They have realized that in some mysterious way physical life and health is closely bound up with the blood supply and the purity thereof. This thought is expressed in countless aphorisms, of which the one quoted at the head of this lesson ("The Blood is the Life") is a typical example.

In view of the facts of the case, it is amazing that the average person has but the slightest conception of the offices of the blood, and the processes of the circulation of the blood. The average man does not grasp the idea that the blood is filled with the nourishment extracted from the food, and that the circulation of the blood is largely concerned with the distribution of this nourishment. Instead, he has a general hazy idea that the nourishment is "soaked up" by the system from the stomach in some unknown and mysterious way. He realizes that his blood is an important item of his physical well-being, and that if it is weak, or if he loses it, he weakens or dies—but this is about as far as his thought of the subject extends.

I have found it advisable to inform patients on this point, because when they grasp the idea their minds seem to take up the suggestion more clearly, and they unconsciously co-operate with the efforts of the practitioner to bring about improved nutrition of all parts of the body. The suggestion of **"rich red blood, flowing to all parts of the body, building up and strengthening it, repairing and creating it anew,"** is one of the greatest value in many cases. The patient easily, and involuntarily, makes a mental picture of the desired condition, which, of course, is then objectified in his physical condition according to the rule that "mental ideas take form in physical conditions."

Let us then carefully study the processes of the circulation of the blood, and the offices and functions of the blood, that we may hold the right kind of mental pictures ourselves, and thus be able to convey the same to the mind of the patient in our work of treatment.

The Blood is the red fluid which circulates through the arteries and veins of man and the higher animals. It is formed from the Chyle and Lymph when these substances are subjected to the action of the oxygen taken into the lungs by the process of inspiration. It is the general material from which all of the secretions of the body are derived. In the blood current is also carried away from the different parts of the body various noxious debris and waste products of the system, which are thus carried to the crematory of the lungs, there to be burned up by the oxygen therein, and then eliminated from the system in the form of carbonic-acid gas.

"THE BLOOD IS THE LIFE"

Blood has a salty taste, and when fresh it has a peculiar odor. It is composed of about seventy-eight per cent of water; about six or seven per cent of albumen; about thirteen per cent of coloring matter; and a small percentage each of fibrine, crystallizable fat, fluid fat, and various mineral chemicals such as sodium and potassium chlorides, carbonates, phosphates, and sulphates, and calcium and magnesium carbonates, phosphates of calcium magnesium and iron, ferric oxide, etc. Under microscopic examination it is seen as a colorless liquid with many minute round red blood corpuscles floating in it, and a smaller number of larger discs called "white corpuscles" moving in its substance. The idea of the real nature of the blood may be grasped from the following statement of an authority on physiology who says: "The blood is the immediate pabulum, or nourishment and sustenance, of the tissues. Its composition is practically identical with that of the tissues; in fact, **it is really liquid flesh."**

The vessels which conduct the blood outward from the heart are known as Arteries; and those which conduct it back to the heart are known as Veins. The blood in the arteries (called "arterial blood") is of a bright red color, while that in the veins (called "venous blood") is of a dark, dull, blackish-purple color. Arterial blood is highly charged with oxygen; venous blood is deoxidized, or lacking in oxygen. We shall see the reason for this difference in the two kinds of blood, or rather the two conditions of the blood (for it is really all the same blood appearing in two conditions or states) when we now study the office of the blood, and the processes of the circulation thereof.

The nourishment of the food is taken into the blood by absorption from the organs of digestion, as we have seen in the lesson on these processes. It reaches the heart and is then sent forward to all parts of the body in the current of rich, red arterial blood which has just been freshly oxygenated by the lungs, as we shall see presently. It is carried to all parts of the body, where it is eagerly taken up by the various class and tissues, and by them is converted into new cell-substance, and tissue-substance, and built into flesh, muscle, and tissue in general. The body needs this new material in order to replace that which has broken down and been discarded; and also to repair the remaining tissue-substance.

The blood returning to the heart in the condition of dark, dirty venous blood carries with it the garbage and debris of the system, the particles of broken down cells and tissue, and other impurities of the system, which, if left in the system, would poison it. This debris is bound for the crematory of the lungs, where it is burned up by the oxygen inspired in the act of breathing, and is then cast forth in the form of carbonic-acid gas.

Before proceeding to a consideration of the process of the lungs, however, let us stop for a moment to view that wonderful instrument, the Heart. The Heart is a hollow, pear-shaped organ, about the size of an average clenched fist. It is situated on the left-hand side of the body, between the two lungs. It is divided into four compartments, of which the two upper are called **auricles,** and the two lower called **ventricles.** The auricles have veins opening into them; the ventricles have arteries arising from them.

The returning venous blood reaches the right auricle; when the latter is filled to its capacity its walls contract and expel the blood through an opening into the right ventricle; this in turn contracts and forces the blood through the pulmonary artery into the lungs (there to undergo a process which we shall consider presently). After the processes of the lungs have been performed, the blood is forced back into the left auricle of the heart, which in turn forces it into the left ventricle. The left ventricle then forces the blood out into the arteries through the aorta, which latter is the largest artery of the system.

The arterial system carries forward the blood-current, first through the main arteries and then through the divisions and subdivisions thereof, ending in the tiny hair-like capillaries which reach to every cell and cell group in the body. The blood having given up such part of its nourishment as is needed at the moment, and having transferred a tiny particle of oxygen to such points where it is needed, then starts on its return journey to the lungs, this time taking the route of the **veins,** for it is now venous blood, dark, dull, lacking in oxygen, and filled with impurities. It starts back first through the capillaries of the venous system, then passing on to the smaller veins, and then to the larger, and then to the main veins which pour it into the right auricle (as previously stated), from which it is passed via the right ventricle and the pulmonary artery into the lungs, there to be purified and oxygenated.

To many it seems strange to include the lungs when considering the subject of the circulation of the blood; but in a moment we shall see that the sole offices of the lungs are the performance of the work of cleansing and oxygenating the blood—without this there would be no need of lungs at all. Yet so ignorant is the general person of the principles of physiology that the lungs seem utterly devoid of any connection with the blood, and from any functions to be performed in the direction indicated. There is great need for public instruction on this point—for knowledge here certainly spells H-e-a-l-t-h to mankind.

The Lungs are two in number, and are located in the upper part of the trunk, in that part of the body commonly called "the chest." They are separated from each other by the heart, and its great blood-vessels, and the larger air tubes. The trachea, or windpipe, conveys the inspired air to the lungs; at its lower end it divides into the bronchial tubes which enter the lungs. The bronchial tubes then divide and subdivide into smaller tubes, like the branches and twigs of a tree, until they terminate into tiny lobules, or oval sacs or bags. These lobules or air-spaces in the lungs are very small and very numerous; it is estimated that there are many millions of them in each lung. It has been estimated that if these air cells of the lungs were spread out on a plane surface they would extend over an area of nearly fifteen thousand square feet.

These tiny air-cells are enmeshed in an intricate network of tiny capillaries of the circulatory system, which are filled with venous blood just returned from the various parts of the system to the lungs, there to be purified and oxygenated. It is estimated that about 35,000 pints of blood traverse or pass through these capillaries each twenty-four hours, **the blood corpuscles passing in single file through these tiny capillary canals, each being exposed to a tiny particle of air on each side of the canals.**

When the blood corpuscle comes in contact with the air in the lungs, as just stated, the oxygen in the air penetrates the coating of the coverings, and, coming into direct contact with the blood, oxygenation and a process of chemical combustion takes place. In this process the oxygen "burns up" the filthy waste matter in the venous blood and converts it into carbonic-acid gas which is then thrown out of the lungs in the expiring breath. And, at the same time the blood takes up tiny particles of oxygen which it carries to all parts of the system, where it is used in certain important processes in connection with the cells and tissues—it serving to strengthen and invigorate, renovate and repair, every cell and tissue. Arterial blood carries with it about twenty-five per cent of pure oxygen.

Not only does the oxygen in the blood perform the office above mentioned, but it also materially aids in certain processes of digestion which depends upon a proper oxygenation. The combustion arising from the contact of the oxygen with the waste substances also generates heat, and equalizes the temperature of the body.

In addition to the system cf blood-circulation, there is another very important system existing and operating in co-operation with the former. This secondary system is called the Lymphatic System. Lymph closely resembles Blood in its composition. It is composed of some of the ingredients of the blood which have exuded from the walls of the blood-vessels, and also of some of the waste materials of the system which require "making over." The lymphatic system attends to this repair work, and also several other functions of the system. The renovated waste-material is passed once more into the blood, there to be used by the system. The lymph circulates in thin, very delicate tubes, which are invisible to the unaided human eye—they may be injected with quicksilver, however, and thus made visible. These lymphatic tubes empty into several of the large veins, the lymph mingling with the returning venous blood, and thus reaching the lungs and heart in due course. Certain portions of the food-nourishment reach the lymphatic system from the intestines, and there undergo certain transforming processes before entering the blood-supply proper.

So, we see the importance of the blood in the work of body-building and body-maintaining. **The blood in one's body constitutes one-tenth of his entire weight.** Of this amount about one-quarter is distributed in the heart, lungs, large arteries and veins; about one-quarter in the liver; about one-quarter in the muscles; the remaining one-quarter being distributed among the other organs and tissues; the brain utilizing about one-fifth of the entire quantity of blood in the system.

It is seen without argument that the general health of a person depends materially upon his supply of blood being adequate, rich, and sufficiently well oxygenated. The richness of the blood depends, of course, upon the work of the organs of nutrition; its oxygenation depends upon the work of the lungs; and its normal action upon the work of the heart and the arterial and venous system. All of these organs are amenable to mental treatment along the general lines laid down in these lessons.

The lungs are quite receptive to mental treatment, and respond by displaying greater strength and activity, particularly when aided by the cultivation of the habit of proper breathing, which habit most persons have lost. The heart and the, arterial and venous systems respond readily to mental treatment. So true is this that strong positive mental suggestion will increase the circulation to any one part to which the attention and treatment is directed—this may be proved by actual experiment. The action of the heart has been found to respond to properly directed suggestion—this also is capable of being proved by experiment, though one should not experiment idly with this organ. The heart is the most intelligent and sensitive of all the organs of the body. It responds to loving, careful suggestions and advice—but must never be driven or abused.

LESSON XXV

THE REPRODUCTIVE SYSTEM

As we have seen in previous lessons, Nature has as her two principal ends (1) the preservation and maintenance of the body of the individual being, in health, vigor, and normal functioning; and (2) the perpetuation and preservation of the race. The first end is served by means of the processes of vital activity, such as we have just considered; the second end is served by the processes of generation and reproduction, the system of which we shall now consider. Self-preservation and the instinct of sex and parenthood—these two constitute Nature's primal and elementary instincts; and she has built up and maintained an intricate and elaborate mechanism to serve her purposes in both of these instinctive series of processes.

The reproductive organism of the male human being is as follows: (1) The Penis; (2) the Testes; (3) the Prostate Gland; (4) the Cowper's Glands; (5) the Vesiculae Seminales. The following brief somewhat technical description gives a general idea of the characteristics and functions of each of these.

The Penis is the intromittent reproductive organ of the male; that is to say, the organ by and through which the seminal fluid is conveyed from the male to the female reproductive organism. This organ consists of erectile tissue arranged in three cylindrical compartments, each

203

of which is surrounded by a fibrous sheath. It consists of several parts, which are called the roots, the body, and the extremity or glans penis, respectively. It is also surrounded by vessels, nerves, and skin.

The Testes, or testicles, are two glands which secrete the seminal fluid of the male. They are egg-shaped, and are suspended in the scrotum or pouch by means of the spermatic cords. A short, closely contracted scrotum is generally regarded as a sign of the health of the reproductive organism, and of the general system; while an elongated, flabby scrotum is regarded as a sign of physical depression and lack of vigor. Nature protects the testes by six separate coverings, the two outer ones of which are the muscles and skin of the scrotum. The spermatic cord is composed of arteries, veins, lymphatics, nerves, and the excretory ducts of the testes, and extend from the internal abdominal ring to the back part of the testicles which it supports in the scrotum.

The Prostate Gland is a muscular gland located in front of the neck of the bladder, and at the beginning of the urethra or canal which carries the urine from the bladder, and which in the male also carries the seminal fluid. This gland resembles a horse-chestnut in shape and size. It secretes a milky fluid which passes through the prostatic ducts into the prostatic portion of the urethra. In middle-aged men this organ sometimes becomes enlarged and troublesome, but this condition may be removed by the proper treatment.

The Cowper's Glands are two small glands, about the size of peas, situated one on each side of the membraneous portion of the urethra, close above the bulb, each gland having an excretory opening into the bulbous portion of the urethra.

The Vesiculae Seminales, or seminal vesicles, are two small pouches lying between the rectum and the base of the bladder; they serve as reservoirs for the semen, and also for another fluid which accompanies the semen in its discharge. It has two ejaculatory ducts, one on each side.

The Semen, or seminal fluid (containing the reproductive "seed") is secreted by the testes, and stored in the reservoirs of the vesiculae seminales above described. It consists of a colorless transparent fluid, in which is contained solid particles of protoplasm, namely the seminal granules and the spermatozoa. Under sexual excitement the semen is forced from the vesiculae seminales by muscular contraction, and, passing into the urethra is met by the secretions of the Cowper's Glands, and those of certain mucous follicles opening into the urethral passages; peristaltic action finally ejaculating the seminal fluid from the male organism. The spermatozoa are the essential element of the seminal fluid, the other fluids and secretions being merely accessory and secondary in function and offices.

The Spermatozoa, or male elements of reproduction, are microscopic living creatures, each resembling a minute tadpole, with head, rod-like body, and a hair-like tail which is in constant motion from side to side, the tail serving to propel the creature to its destination. In the male human being the spermatozoa each measure about one six-hundredth of an inch in length, and are present in countless numbers in the semen. They dwell in the gelatinous mass which composes a part of the seminal fluid of the male. The spermatozoa constitute the so-called "seed" of the male, which impregnates the ovum of the female, as we shall see presently.

The reproductive organism of the female human being is grouped into two classes, viz., the external organs, and the internal organs, respectively.

The external reproductive organism of the female human being is as follows: (1) The Mons Veneris, or fatty eminence in front of the pubis, above the other external organs; (2) the Labia Majora and the Labia Minora, being respectively the large and small lip-like coverings enclosing and protecting the vaginal orifice; (3) the Clitoris, a small organ hidden by the labia minora, having at its extremity a small sensitive tubercle; (4) the Meatus Urinarius, or orifice of the urethra of the female, which lies near to the vagina and about an inch below the clitoris —this, strictly speaking however, is not a reproductive organ although associated with such, as its purpose is that of serving as a passage for the urine; (5) the Vaginal Orifice is the outer entrance to the vagina, and is located just below the meatus urinarius. It is surrounded by the sphincter vaginae muscle.

The internal reproductive organism of the human female is composed of the following organs: (1) The Vagina, a canal or channel leading from the vaginal orifice to the uterus or womb, which is situated in front of the rectum and behind the bladder. It extends in an upward and backward curve of about six inches in length, and reaches and encloses the lower part of the neck of the uterus or womb. On either side of the vagina, near the orifice, are the two glands of Bartholine, which correspond closely to the Cowper's glands of the male, with excretory ducts opening upon the side of the labia minora. The vagina is lined with a muscular coat, a layer of erectile tissue, and an internal mucous lining. It is capable of great distension in childbirth, after which it resumes its normal dimensions. The office of the vagina is to serve as a channel for the introduction of the fertilizing male seminal fluid; to sustain the weight of the uterus; to serve as a passage for the menstrual fluid; and to afford a passage for the delivery of the infant at childbirth.

(2) The Uterus, or womb, is a hollow pear-shaped muscular organ, about three inches long, two inches broad, and one inch thick. It is the organ of gestation which receives the fecundated ovum in its cavity, and supports and retains the foetus during its development. The upper and broader part is called the fundus; the lower contracted portion being called the cervix,

or neck, which projects into the vagina. The uterus is composed of a muscular coat, which contracts as do the walls of the stomach and bladder; this coat extends very greatly during the period of pregnancy. The uterus is located just behind and slightly above the bladder, and is supported by eight ligaments which, when in a healthy condition, hold it firmly and easily in place. Displacement of the uterus is caused by the weakening or relaxing of some of these ligaments—this condition may be relieved and cured by proper treatment in the direction of strengthening the ligaments by suggestions directed to that end.

(3) The Fallopian Tubes are the ducts of the ovaries which serve to convey the ova from the ovaries to the cavity in the uterus; they are two in number, one on each side, each tube being about four inches in length. They extend from either side of the fundus of the womb until they communicate with the ovaries.

(4) The Ovaries are two oval-shaped organs lying one on each side of the uterus; the ova are formed in them, and they correspond to the testes in the male. They are about one and one-half inches long, one inch wide, and one-half inch in thickness. They are covered with a dense, firm coating which encloses a soft fibrous tissue, abundantly supplied with blood-vessels, which is called the stroma. Imbedded in the mesh-like tissue of the stroma are numerous small, round transparent vesicles, in various stages of development, known as the Graafian follicles,

which are lined with a layer of peculiar granular cells. These follicles are the receptacles or sacs which contain the ova or eggs which constitute the female reproductive germ; each vesicle containing a single ovum, or egg.

(5) The Ovum, or egg, of the human female is a very small round body measuring from one two-hundred-and-fiftieth of an inch to one one-hundred-and-twentieth of an inch in diameter. It is surrounded with a transparent colorless envelope in which is contained the yolk consisting of globules of various sizes; the center of the yolk consisting of a thin transparent vesicle which in turn contains a tiny granular, opaque, yellow structure known as "the germinal spot." This ovum, or egg, is discharged and enters the uterus at the menstrual period. When this period arrives the Graafian follicle becomes enlarged by reason of the accumulation of the fluids in its interior, and exerts such a steady and increasing pressure from within, outward, that the surrounding tissue yields with it, and it finally protrudes from the ovary and is then expelled from it with a gush. Following this rupture there occurs a hemorrhage from the vesicles of the follicle, the cavity being filled with blood which then coagulates and is retained in the Graafian follicle. The formation and development of the Graafian follicles begin at puberty and continues until the menopause or change of life in the woman. The ripening and discharge of the eggs produce a peculiar condition of congestion of the entire female generative

organism, including the Fallopian tubes, uterus, vagina, etc.

Menstruation is the "monthly flow" of bloody fluid from the uterus which occurs in all healthy (but non-pregnant) women from puberty until the menopause or "change of life." Puberty is the age at which a woman begins her period of possible child-bearing. In temperate climates the average age is about fourteen years, while in tropical climes puberty occurs a year or two earlier, and in arctic zones a year or two later. The menopause or "change of life" in woman is the beginning of her period of non-reproductiveness; this time is reached when the woman is about forty-five years of age, on the average, although in some cases it is reached several years later, and in a few cases a little earlier. The general rule is that a woman's child-bearing possibility extends over a period of thirty years, on the average. At the time of the menopause, and after, the ovaries diminish in size, the Graafian follicles cease to form and develop, the Fallopian tubes atrophy, and other physical changes manifest themselves.

Menstruation, when once fully established, occurs at intervals of every twenty-eight days on the average in the case of healthy women; in some cases, however, it occurs as often as every twenty-one days, while in others it occurs as seldom as every six weeks, without effecting the general health or normal functioning. Menstruation ceases temporarily during pregnancy, and also usually is inhibited during the period of nursing. The menstrual flow continues for about four or five days, on the average; although here too there is a wide range of variation from the average. The flow increases during the first part of the period, and decreases during the last part. Menstruation is accompanied by the congestion previously noted, and a sense of physical discomfort and irritable emotional feeling. Menstruation is accompanied by a hypertrophy of the mucous membrane of the uterus, and later by a shedding of this hypertrophied membrane, which leaves the underlying vessels exposed and bleeding. After the period new mucous membrane is formed. As before stated, the ovum is discharged and enters the uterus at this period.

The ovum, unless impregnated by a spermatazoon of the male, gradually loses its vitality and is thrown out of the system; if impregnated, however, it remains attached to the walls of the uterus and in time develops into the fœtus. The ovum contains all the rudiments of the young creature, but unless it is impregnated and fertilized by the spermatazoon it never develops. The impregnated ovum begins to form a segmentation-nucleus, and then the segmentation or "spitting up" process begins, and new cells rapidly form. There appears an opaque streak known as "the primitive trace" of the embryo, and the young living creature begins its life history. The period of gestation continues for about nine solar months, or about two hundred and eighty days, although in exceptional cases it continues for but seven months, and in others even as long as ten months.

The reproductive organism of both man and woman is very responsive to suggestion and mental treatment along the lines indicated in these lessons. Weakened parts may be materially strengthened by the proper suggestions intelligently directed. In the case of weakness of the uterus, falling of the womb, etc., a line of suggestions directed toward the strengthening and contraction of the supporting ligaments and muscles will be found very effective. The uterus is very sensitive to mental treatment, and is much like the heart in its degree of "intelligence" and responsiveness. There is a great field for scientific mental treatment here, and one in which medical science has failed to afford the best results—too often the surgeon's knife has been used needlessly. The skilled practitioner of mental healing who specializes upon this class of cases should obtain wonderful results, thereby performing a worthy work and at the same time establishing himself or herself in a paying practice.

LESSON XXVI

"WHEN THE HAND OF THE POTTER SLIPS"

In many oriental poems, such as the "Rubaiyat" of Omar Khayyam, there is found a reference to the favorite oriental analogy of the Potter and the Pots—the Creative Power being the Potter, and the human creature being the Pot which has been molded by the hand of the Potter. When a diseased or deformed body is seen, then it is said that "the hand of the Potter slipped." And, indeed, this figurative picture is in close resemblance to the truth; for the hand of Nature at times does seem to "slip" in its work, although in many cases the slip is caused by an interference of the human creature with Nature's own well-laid plans and established machinery of operation. Nature being in this case merely the Corporeal Mind, it is seen that the slip is one of that wonderful mental organization, and one which may at least, to a great extent, be remedied by appealing direct to it, as in the case of scientific Mental Healing as set forth in these lessons.

While have said that I did not purpose holding before the minds of my students any pictures of diseased conditions, yet for the purpose of aiding them in their work of practicing Mental Healing I have thought it well to present in this lesson a general classification of the ways in which "the hand of the Potter slips," in order that the practitioner may see clearly and plainly the nature of the task of reparative work which he must impose upon the Corporeal Mind (in some of its phases) to perform, so that the patient may regain health, strength and normal functioning. It will, of course, be understood that the following is not a complete list of physical ailments, nor is it a lesson on pathology. It is merely a general classification, with general suggestions as to treatment of the "slips" in such class.

General Treatment. In most cases it will be found well for the practitioner to give the new patient a General Treatment, i. e., a treatment for general physical health and strength. This is accomplished by treating each general function or activity of the body in turn, beginning with the main organs of nutrition, then proceeding to the organs of elimination, and then the organs of circulation, the heart and the arteries and veins, etc., not forgetting the lungs in this connection. Then follow with the reproductive system, and then the muscles, joints, etc. In this way a general improvement of the whole system is started under way, and a firm foundation thus laid for subsequent special or local treatments for specific complaints. In very many cases, as I have said elsewhere in these lessons, such a General Treatment, particularly the treatment of the main organs of nutrition and elimination, will cure the patient of his local and specific complaint, the latter being really but a symptom of the main trouble which has been removed. A patient in whom perfect nutrition and perfect elimination is effected generally manages to throw off the special complaint without much more trouble. The practitioner will do well to always bear this fact in mind, for it will explain many strange and rapid cures, and will also "give him a line" on the course of treatment in many puzzling cases which have defied other kinds of treatment.

Troubles of the Organs of Nutrition. The chief troubles in this class are mal-nutrition (imperfect nourishment), and dyspepsia, indigestion, etc.; these several troubles usually being associated and existing at the same time. The course of treatment here is obvious, i. e., treatment should be directed toward energizing the stomach and intestines into activity and normal functioning. The stomach should be urged to perform its work properly, and the patient should be instructed to furnish it with wholesome food only; the small intestine should be urged to resume normal functioning, and to aid in the work of digestion and assimilation, in order that there may be created rich nourishing blood which will build up the entire system. The stomach of a dyspeptic is generally found to be in **a state of panic**—this must be relieved by proper suggestions, and confidence restored. The stomach and intestines are quite intelligent, and will respond quickly to the right kind of suggestion.

The Liver, **as** I have said, is a stupid, slow,

stubborn organ, and requires the most vigorous and positive kind of suggestions, orders, commands and general "scolding" in order to be made to resume normal functioning. It must be approached in a positive mental attitude, much the same in which one would approach a pig, mule, or goat—mastery must be asserted and maintained. A little actual practice will show the practitioner the best line of suggestions and commands to use in such cases—but the general rule is to **be firm and positive in dealing with the liver.**

Troubles of the Organs of Elimination. The bowels, kidneys, and bladder are quite receptive to suggestion, and will respond to and co-operate with the efforts of the practitioner who approaches them in the right spirit and manner. There is but one general rule, and that is to tell the organ plainly and kindly just what is required of it, and how it must behave itself. Train it just as you would an intelligent dog. You will be surprised at first to see how rapidly and intelligently the organ will respond. In the case of constipation, the patient should be instructed to make and keep his or her engagement with the bowels each day, i. e. to go to stool at a set time whether or not an inclination is felt. The bowels will quickly respond to this confidence, and will be felt to be actually and earnestly endeavoring to keep its part of the agreement. Where purgative medicines have been employed, and the pill habit established, it will take a longer time than otherwise to neutralize this old habit and to establish the new and normal one. Tendency to urinate too often may be checked by the proper suggestions, and the muscles controlling the bladder may be taught to contract tighter and to maintain the contraction better and longer. The words **"tighten"** or **"loosen,"** respectively convey a strong suggestion to this class of muscles—the sphincter muscles which surround, and by their contraction tend to close, the various openings of the organs of elimination. In treating diarrhea and "loose bowels," simply reverse the suggestions given in the case of constipation, of course.

Troubles of the Heart and Circulation. The heart, and the arteries and veins, are very amenable to suggestion, and will respond very intelligently to it when properly given. As I have stated elsewhere in these lessons, the heart is very gentle and intelligent—the very reverse of the liver—and should be treated accordingly. It is like a gentle, high-spirited, well-bred horse, or like an intelligent gentle child, in its mental character and make-up. Rough methods or treatment should be avoided in treating the heart or the circulatory system in general; gentle, kindly, soothing words and tones, and clear, plain, intelligent directions should be given it. You may even (and often very effectively) explain to the heart the trouble that is being caused by imperfect action, accompanying the explanation with suggestions as to how the trouble may be overcome, and new and better habits of actions acquired. In case of cold hands or feet, you may direct an increased circulation to those parts by calling the attention of the circulatory system mind to the matter. Anaemia, or deficient blood supply, is of course to be treated by improving the nutrition; for the heart cannot furnish nourishment to the blood, nor the blood to the parts of the body, unless it has been assimilated and absorbed from the food eaten by the patient. Dropsy, or an abnormal accumulation of serum, which causes swelling, etc., may be treated by stimulating the kidneys and the skin to carry off the excess fluids, and to thereafter perform their functions normally.

Troubles of the Lungs. The lungs respond very well to suggestions properly directed. The suggestion should be along the lines of increased activity and resistance. The cells should be urged to greater efforts, and taught to resist invading organisms. In cases of this kind, it will be found well to pay attention to the organs of nutrition also, for it is a fact that a well-nourished body is better able to fight off and defeat attacking organisms. The patient should be taught the value of correct breathing, for the exercise of the lungs is often sufficient to prevent or to overcome weakness thereof.

Rheumatic Troubles. Rheumatism is a condition arising from imperfect circulation and imperfect elimination; therefore, by treating both of these conditions the special trouble tends to disappear.

Troubles of the Sense-Organs. Weakness of sight, hearing, or smell may be treated by building up the general system, by providing proper nutrition and elimination; and also by special energizing treatment directed to the seat of the trouble. The cells may be energized into more normal functioning, by an appeal directed immediately to them. The patient may aid materially in such treatment, by directing his or her **attention** to the organ in question, and maintaining a mental attitude of **expectant attention.** This use of the mind of the patient, encouraged and supplemented by that of your own mind, will often bring marked and rapid results. Sense organs are very responsive to increased demands made upon them by their owner, particularly if the owner manifests a mental state of **confident expectation**—the organ seems to realize that better work is expected of it, and it tries to "make good"; reversing the rule, the organ seems to realize distrust and lack of confidence in it, and responds in like measure.

Neuralgic Troubles, Headaches, etc. Neuralgic troubles, headaches, etc., usually arise from imperfect nutrition, or imperfect elimination, or both, although in some cases there is found a condition of imperfect circulation. The treatment is obvious, when the cause is perceived.

The direction of the mind and the suggestions to the local parts however often relieve the immediate distress; but the healer should never be satisfied until he has removed the root of the trouble as well as the local symptoms.

Reproductive Complaints. The troubles of the male and female reproductive organism may be effectively treated by suggestion and mental treatment scientifically and intelligently applied. In the case of weakness of the male reproductive organism, mental treatment may be applied in the direction of a general energizing of the whole system, which is far more simple than in the cases of women. In cases of weakness of the male, treatment may also be effectively directed to the lower part of the spinal column, just where the bony parts spread out into a broad flat bone; for certain nerves in this region are closely connected with the male reproductive organism.

In the case of weakness of the female reproductive system, suggestion and mental treatment is usually found very effective; in fact, this is a great field for the scientific practitioner of mental healing, for here he or she obtains some wonderful results. **Displacements of the uterus, falling of the womb, etc., are treated by suggestions to the supporting ligaments and muscles, and orders to them to contract and do better work in the direction of supporting the uterus properly.** These ligaments respond very readily in most cases, and a marked improvement is speedily manifested. The general suggestion in such cases should be based on the mental pattern conveyed by the ideas **"up"** and **"firmly in place,"** respectively. Menstrual troubles may be effectively treated by suggestions directed to the ovaries and uterus, and to the reproductive system in general, the general thought being **"normal and natural action."** Too profuse menses are to be treated by checking the tendency to flow in the same way as diarrhea is checked, i. e. by suggestion of **"slow,"** and **"not so free,"** etc. In all cases of female troubles it is well to build up the general system, particularly the organs of nutrition and elimination. Many cases of uterine troubles originally arise from the presence of a distended, impacted colon —this condition resulting from constipation, etc. When the cause is removed, it is a comparatively simple matter to remedy the local trouble.

Nervous Troubles. What are generally known as "nervous" troubles may be treated by first attending to the organs of nutrition and elimination, and then by a special treatment of the spinal column. In the latter the thought must be swept up and down the spinal column, with the idea held in mind that **the spinal column is being energized, freed from obstructing influences, conditions and tendencies.** In fact, it is a good plan to finish any kind of treatment in this way—the sweeping of the spine acting as a general stimulating influence which is very gratifying and pleasant to the patient.

MENTAL THERAPEUTICS

Another general treatment effective in all cases is that known as "equalizing the circulation," in which the thought sweeps down and then up over the whole body, several times in succession; this tends to energize and equalize the circulation over the entire system, bringing a pleasant tingling to the body of the patient, and resulting in a refreshing sensation and feeling afterward.

Self-Treatment. The student who wishes to heal himself or herself by means of Mental Therapeutics has but to remember that each and every form, method, principle, and rule of treatment given in these lessons for the treatment of the patient is equally valid and applicable in the treatment of oneself. Apply the same treatment, in the same way, and you obtain the same result in Self-Healing. If I were writing a series of lessons on the subject of Self-Healing, I could merely repeat what I have said in these lessons regarding the treatment of other patients. The principle is identical, and the methods of application are practically the same.

In Self-Treatment the "I" part of yourself should act as the practitioner, while the Corporeal Mind of yourself should be the patient. Proceed in such case as if you were really treating another person, the body of another. This is the whole secret in a few words.

Concluding Advice. In all forms of mental treatment, no matter what particular methods you may employ, or what particular trouble you may be treating, you should always carry in mind the fact that THOUGHT is the active principle involved in the cure. And you should learn to think of Thought not as an intangible, unsubstantial thing, but rather as **a great natural energy and force,** something as real as is electricity or magnetism. It will help you to mentally picture it as sweeping from you into the body of the patient, there energizing and strengthening the minds in the cells and parts of that body. The more clearly that you can visualize or mentally picture it as actually travelling and moving like a great current of electricity, the greater will be its potency.

Do not allow yourself to become wrapped up in technical theories or speculations regarding the Riddle of the Universe, or of the inner nature of Mind. Leave these subjects to the metaphysicians who delight in them to such an extent that they usually have no time or inclination to do anything practical in life. Do not be a dreamer, but be a do-er. Cultivate the characteristics of the Constructive Thinker—build-up, construct, create, with the Power of Mind. You will find that your Power to Heal will increase with practice and habit. You will develop what some have called "the sanative contagion," to such an extent that those coming into your presence will receive healing thought even though you do not voluntarily send the same forth; then you will **radiate** healing power —this is the mark of the true healer. Think of yourself as a SUN of HEALING POWER, and let your radiance flow forth in all directions.

You will learn new details of practice every year of your life; but you will always be impressed with the truth of the statement that the Principle of Mental Healing is very simple and plain, when once grasped and understood. Here is a simple statement of this simple fact, to carry with you as my parting gift:

"Mental Patterns are reproduced in Physical States, Forms, and Conditions."

LESSON XXVII

MAGNETIC AND SPIRITUAL HEALING

Although I have finished this course of lessons as originally planned, I have thought it advisable to add to it a brief consideration of two forms of healing which while scientifically included in the broad classification of Mental Therapeutics, nevertheless have some points of difference from the general methods of this system. I refer to (1) Magnetic Healing; and (2) Spiritual Healing, respectively. In these two forms of healing I find the same fundamental principle operative, although called forth and manifested in a different manner. In the following pages I shall endeavor to explain this apparent difference, and at the same time to explain the particular methods employed in each of these general methods; to the end that such of my students who may wish to include these methods in their own practice may be enabled to do so intelligently and effectively.

Magnetic Healing. What is known as "Magnetic Healing" has gained quite a large following in Europe and America, and many wonderful cures have been made by practitioners following this method. In America it is usually applied in connection with the more regular forms of mental healing, while in France it is often practiced as a distinct branch of therapeutics. Those who have carefully investigated the subject of **Magnetic Healing** have generally reached the conclusion that its effects arise from a dual cause, as follows: (a) the energizing effect of a transference of vital energy from the body of the healer to that of the patient; and, (b) accompanying the effect just mentioned, the power of Thought along the lines set forth in these lessons.

I shall not go into the subject of the "vital force" employed in Magnetic Healing, for the subject is not at all well understood even by those practicing and teaching its principles. Enough for the purpose of this consideration is the fact that there undoubtedly exists that which may be called "vital force" in the human body, and which may be transferred to another person under certain conditions; and which when so transferred tends to energize into renewed activity the body of that other person, or any of his physical organs toward which the force may be directed by the healer. It is important in this connection to note that this "vital force" is best directed by the healer when he fixes his attention upon the part of the body of the patient to be treated—this shows that the "vital force" is subordinate to Mind, and is controlled thereby. Those who may wish to inquire into the essential nature of this "vital force" may obtain interesting information by studying the oriental teac,ings concerning what is called "prana," which is practically identical with what we of the western world call "vital force."

Nearly all nations in the history of the race

have employed some phase of this form of healing with effect—and in most cases we may see
that they also, consciously or unconsciously, employed mental suggestion or thought-force in
such treatments. The "laying on of hands" has
always been a popular form of treatment, and
many good results have arisen therefrom. But
we must never lose sight of the fact that in such
processes **the minds both of the patient and of
the healer have been directed to the affected part**
—the effect of which may be easily understood
by those who have carefully studied the lessons
of this course. The healer, and the patient, both
understood that the treatment was expected to
produce certain effects; and both naturally and
instinctively pictured the expected result—**and
so obtained it.**

Outside of the effect of the "vital force" upon
the patient (whatever the degree of that effect
may really be when divorced from the mental
effect of the thought of practitioner and patient)
there is undoubtedly a strong suggestive effect
in the application of the hands to the affected
part, or the placing of them near the region affected. **The eye sees the motion, and the body
feels the contact,** and both of these elements add
materially to the suggestive value of the treatment. The mere tapping of the region of the
liver by the fingers of the healer, serves to arouse
the mind in the liver and to make it attentive to
the suggestions given it mentally—it is akin to
tapping on the shoulder of a man to whom you
wish to speak; or to rapping on the door of a

man's room, when you wish to arouse his attention.

Longitudinal passes made downward over the body of a reclining patient will tend to increase his circulation, and to equalize it. Downward passes have a soothing effect as a rule; while upward passes have an awakening, arousing effect. Transversal passes made sidewise across the body of the patient will tend to "loosen up" the action of the organs in that location. A twisting or "boring" motion of the extended finger will often rouse into activity sluggish organs; a feeling of warmth often accompanying this result. Pain may be removed by an application of the palms of the hands to the affected part. Stroking the body, or a part thereof, with the tips of the fingers often has a soothing effect. Rubbing a sore spot, such as a rheumatic joint, usually benefits it. Some practitioners employ a "vibrational motion," or shaking motion to the body of the patient, claiming good results therefrom. Hot Insufflation, or breathing upon the affected part through a handkerchief or napkin often brings relief from pain.

If you should see fit to combine this form of treatment with your Mental Healing proper, I advise you to always keep in mind the effect of the Mind even in such treatments, and to add all of your regular Mental Healing methods to that of the "Magnetic Healing." For in this way you obtain whatever benefit or virtue there may be in the Magnetic Treatment, while at the same time not losing the effect of your Mental

Healing methods. Finally, I freely admit that in the case of certain patients who have been strongly impressed with the theory of "Magnetism," the use of the hands in the treatment greatly adds to the efficacy of the mental treatment.

Govern yourself according to circumstances, and be prepared to give to the patient that which is most readily accepted by him; the reason for this I have made plain in the earlier lessons of this course.

Spiritual Healing. While in my judgment the essence of what is called "spiritual treatment" is to be found in the ideas in the mind of the patient, or of the healer, rather than in some super-mental force, nevertheless I feel that the student should become acquainted with the general theory and form of practice of this phase of healing, so that he may combine the same with his other methods, or else practice it solely, if he should see fit. Whatever else there is or is not in Spiritual Healing, there certainly is a powerful suggestive force in it, particularly when the mind of the patient is inclined to run along those particular lines. Personally, I do not claim to be a Spiritual Healer, or a teacher thereof; but I have a sufficiently extended knowledge of the subject to be able to select the best methods of applying the same. And, while I cannot attempt to go into the matter deeply in this lesson, yet I below present to you a brief comprehensive synopsis of the gist of the best teaching on the subject, and also give you one or two very good forms of administering this form of treatment.

The essence of the theory of Spiritual Healing of the highest order is this: That man is capable of raising the vibrations of his consciousness up above that of his ordinary plane of consciousness, and to thereby attain "spiritual consciousness." When the healer reaches this plane of consciousness, and pronounces his Healing Word from that plane, he reaches the similar plane of "spiritual consciousness" in the patient, and causes it to manifest its healing power. This spiritual consciousness of the patient is held to be dominant over the lower planes of his mind; and, therefore, when it is aroused, the curative work is performed within his body by the action of his mental and spiritual forces. The plane of "spiritual consciousness," it is held, closely approaches the plane of the Infinite Power which governs all created life; and by thus bringing the patient into nearer contact with this transcendent principle of being, it enables him to receive its beneficent power in the direction of restoring Health.

The following two forms of treatment along the lines of Spiritual Healing are those advised by a high authority on transcendental subjects, and, as will be seen, contain very high statements and principles; in fact, one must be very material indeed who does not experience a feeling of uplift from the mere serious repetition of the words thereof. I herewith submit the same to your attention, without further comment. They are both intended for the use of the healer in raising him up to the plane of "spiritual consciousness," from which he may speak the Healing Word bidding the patient be whole and well.

The first Statement of Spiritual Consciousness is as follows:

"O Spirit—the One, Birthless, Deathless—the Omniscient, Omnipresent, Omnipotent Being— in whose Ocean of Life I am a drop—let me feel thy Presence and Power. Let me realize even more fully what Thou art, and what I am in Thee. Let the consciousness of thy Reality, and my Reality in Thee, permeate my being, and descend upon all the places of my mind. Let the Power of Spirit manifest through my mind, permeating the body of this person that I am desirous of healing (or 'this body that I call mine own,' if you are healing yourself) bringing to it Health and Strength and Life, that it be rendered a more fitting Temple of the Spirit— a more perfect instrument of Expression for the One Life that flows through it. Raise up this body from the gross vibrations of the lower planes, to the higher vibrations of the Spiritual Consciousness, through which and by which we know Thee. Give this body, through the Spiritual Consciousness which is imminent within it, that Peace, and Strength, and Life, that is its by virtue of thy immanence within it. Do Thou, the All-Life, flow in thy essence through this thy reflection and expression, revivifying and enlivening it. This do I claim, O All-Spirit, by virtue of my eternal Birthright from Thee. And, by reason of thy promise and the inner knowledge of the same given to me, I now demand this of Thee!''

The second Statement of Spiritual Consciousness is as follows:

''O thou Great Infinite Power—thou Great Flame of Life of which I am but a spark—I open myself to thy Healing Power, that it may flow through me to strengthen, build-up, and make whole this brother (or sister) in Life. Let thy Power flow through me to the end that he (or she) may receive thy vivifying energy and Strength and Life, and be able to manifest the same as Health, Strength, and Vigor. Make me a worthy channel of thy Power, and use me for Good.''

And, so, my students, I pass on these lessons to you. May you study them carefully, and apply the principles thereof to the best advantage in the healing of those in whom ''the hand of the Potter has slipped.'' Be true to the best within you; manifest the highest power within you—think Health, see Health, preach Health, and you will manifest Health in yourself and those who come to you for help and cure. Do not prostitute your knowledge for selfish motives, or unworthy gain. Be true to your science, and you will be true to yourself and to your patients.

WS - #0175 - 080724 - C0 - 229/152/14 - PB - 9780259895312 - Gloss Lamination